THE FIRESIDE CHATS

FRANKLIN DELANO ROOSEVELT

THE FIRESIDE CHATS

BIBLIOBAZAAR

THE FIRESIDE CHATS

Radio addresses to the
American people broadcast
between 1933 and 1944.

March 12, 1933.

I want to talk for a few minutes with the people of the United States about banking—with the comparatively few who understand the mechanics of banking but more particularly with the overwhelming majority who use banks for the making of deposits and the drawing of checks. I want to tell you what has been done in the last few days, why it was done, and what the next steps are going to be. I recognize that the many proclamations from state capitols and from Washington, the legislation, the treasury regulations, etc., couched for the most part in banking and legal terms should be explained for the benefit of the average citizen. I owe this in particular because of the fortitude and good temper with which everybody has accepted the inconvenience and hardships of the banking holiday. I know that when you understand what we in Washington have been about I shall continue to have your cooperation as fully as I have had your sympathy and help during the past week.

First of all let me state the simple fact that when you deposit money in a bank the bank does not put the money into a safe deposit vault. It invests your money in many different forms of credit—bonds, commercial paper, mortgages and many other kinds of loans. In other words, the bank puts your money to work to keep the wheels of industry and of agriculture turning around. A comparatively small part of the money you put into the bank is kept in currency—an amount which in normal times is wholly sufficient to cover the cash needs of the average citizen. In other words, the total amount of all the currency in the country is only a small fraction of the total deposits in all of the banks.

What, then, happened during the last few days of February and the first few days of March? Because of undermined confidence on the part of the public, there was a general rush by a large portion of our population to turn bank deposits into currency or gold—a rush so great that the soundest banks could not get enough currency to meet the demand. The reason for this was that on the spur of the moment it was, of course, impossible to sell perfectly sound assets of a bank and convert them into cash except at panic prices far below their real value.

By the afternoon of March 3d scarcely a bank in the country was open to do business. Proclamations temporarily closing them in whole or in part had been issued by the governors in almost all the states.

It was then that I issued the proclamation providing for the nation-wide bank holiday, and this was the first step in the government's reconstruction of our financial and economic fabric.

The second step was the legislation promptly and patriotically passed by the Congress confirming my proclamation and broadening my powers so that it became possible in view of the requirement of time to extend the holiday and lift the ban of that holiday gradually. This law also gave authority to develop a program of rehabilitation of our banking facilities. I want to tell our citizens in every part of the nation that the national Congress—Republicans and Democrats alike—showed by this action a devotion to public welfare and a realization of the emergency and the necessity for speed that it is difficult to match in our history.

The third stage has been the series of regulations permitting the banks to continue their functions to take care of the distribution of food and household necessities and the payment of payrolls.

This bank holiday, while resulting in many cases in great inconvenience, is affording us the opportunity to supply the currency necessary to meet the situation. No sound bank is a dollar worse off than it was when it closed its doors last Monday. Neither is any bank which may turn out not to be in a position for immediate opening. The new law allows the twelve Federal Reserve Banks to issue additional currency on good assets and thus the banks which reopen will be able to meet every legitimate call. The new currency is being sent out by the Bureau of Engraving and Printing in large volume to every part of the country. It is sound currency because it is backed by actual, good assets.

A question you will ask is this: why are all the banks not to be reopened at the same time? The answer is simple. Your government does not intend that the history of the past few years shall be repeated. We do not want and will not have another epidemic of bank failures.

As a result, we start tomorrow, Monday, with the opening of banks in the twelve Federal Reserve Bank cities—those banks which on first examination by the treasury have already been found to be all right. This will be followed on Tuesday by the resumption of all their functions by banks already found to be sound in cities where there are recognized clearing houses. That means about 250 cities of the United states.

On Wednesday and succeeding days banks in smaller places all through the country will resume business, subject, of course, to the government's physical ability to complete its survey. It is necessary that the reopening of banks be extended over a period in order to permit the banks to make applications for necessary loans, to obtain currency needed to meet their requirements and to enable the government to make common sense checkups.

Let me make it clear to you that if your bank does not open the first day you are by no means justified in believing that it will not open. A bank that opens on one of the subsequent days is in exactly the same status as the bank that opens tomorrow.

I know that many people are worrying about state banks not members of the Federal Reserve System. These banks can and will receive assistance from members banks and from the Reconstruction Finance Corporation. These state banks are following the same course as the national banks except that they get their licenses to resume business from the state authorities, and these authorities have been asked by the Secretary of the Treasury to permit their good banks to open up on the same schedule as the national banks. I am confident that the state banking departments will be as careful as the national government in the policy relating to the opening of banks and will follow the same broad policy.

It is possible that when the banks resume a very few people who have not recovered from their fear may again begin withdrawals. Let me make it clear that the banks will take care of all needs—and it is my belief that hoarding during the past week has become an exceedingly unfashionable pastime. It needs no prophet to tell you that when the people find that they can get their money— that they can get it when they want it for all legitimate purposes—the phantom of fear will soon be laid. People will again be glad to have their money where it will be safely taken care of and where they can use it conveniently at any time. I can assure you that it is safer to keep your money in a reopened bank than under the mattress.

The success of our whole great national program depends, of course, upon the cooperation of the public—on its intelligent support and use of a reliable system.

Remember that the essential accomplishment of the new legislation is that it makes it possible for banks more readily to convert their assets into cash than was the case before. More liberal provision has been made for banks to borrow on these assets at the Reserve Banks and more liberal provision has also been made for issuing currency on the security of those good assets. This currency is not fiat currency. It is issued only on adequate security—and every good bank has an abundance of such security.

One more point before I close. There will be, of course, some banks unable to reopen without being reorganized. The new law allows the government to assist in making these reorganizations quickly and effectively and even allows the government to subscribe to at least a part of new capital which may be required.

I hope you can see from this elemental recital of what your government is doing that there is nothing complex, or radical, in the process.

We had a bad banking situation. Some of our bankers had shown themselves either incompetent or dishonest in their handling of the people's funds. They had used the money entrusted to them in speculations and unwise loans. This was, of course, not true in the vast majority of our banks, but it was true in enough of them to shock the people for a time into a sense of insecurity and to put them into a frame of mind where they did not differentiate, but seemed to assume that the acts of a comparative few had tainted them all. It was the government's job to straighten out this situation and do it as quickly as possible—and the job is being performed.

I do not promise you that every bank will be reopened or that individual losses will not be suffered, but there will be no losses that possibly could be avoided; and there would have been more and greater losses had we continued to drift. I can even promise you salvation for some at least of the sorely pressed banks. We shall be engaged not merely in reopening sound banks but in the creation of sound banks through reorganization.

It has been wonderful to me to catch the note of confidence from all over the country. I can never be sufficiently grateful to the people for the loyal support they have given me in their acceptance of the judgment that has dictated our course, even though all our processes may not have seemed clear to them.

After all, there is an element in the readjustment of our financial system more important than currency, more important than gold, and that is the confidence of the people. Confidence and courage are the essentials of success in carrying out our plan. You people must have faith; you must not be stampeded by rumors or guesses. Let us unite in banishing fear. We have provided the machinery to restore our financial system; it is up to you to support and make it work.

It is your problem no less than it is mine. Together we cannot fail.

May 7, 1933.

On a Sunday night a week after my inauguration I used the radio to tell you about the banking crisis and the measures we were taking to meet it. I think that in that way I made clear to the country various facts that might otherwise have been misunderstood and in general provided a means of understanding which did much to restore confidence.

Tonight, eight weeks later, I come for the second time to give you my report; in the same spirit and by the same means to tell you about what we have been doing and what we are planning to do.

Two months ago we were facing serious problems. The country was dying by inches. It was dying because trade and commerce had declined to dangerously low levels; prices for basic commodities were such as to destroy the value of the assets of national institutions such as banks, savings banks, insurance companies, and others. These institutions, because of their great needs, were foreclosing mortgages, calling loans, refusing credit. Thus there was actually in process of destruction the property of millions of people who had borrowed money on that property in terms of dollars which had had an entirely different value from the level of March, 1933. That situation in that crisis did not call for any complicated consideration of economic panaceas or fancy plans. We were faced by a condition and not a theory.

There were just two alternatives: The first was to allow the foreclosures to continue, credit to be withheld and money to go into hiding, and thus forcing liquidation and bankruptcy of banks, railroads and insurance companies and a recapitalizing of all business and all property on a lower level. This alternative meant a continuation of what is loosely called "deflation", the net result of which would have been extraordinary hardships on all property owners and, incidentally, extraordinary hardships on all persons working for wages through an increase in unemployment and a further reduction of the wage scale.

It is easy to see that the result of this course would have not only economic effects of a very serious nature but social results that might bring incalculable harm. Even before I was inaugurated I came to the conclusion that such a policy was too much to ask the American people to bear. It involved not only a further loss of homes, farms, savings and wages but also a loss of spiritual values—the loss of that sense of security for the present and the future so necessary to the peace and contentment of the individual and of his family. When you destroy these things you will find it difficult to establish confidence of any sort in the future. It was clear that mere appeals from Washington for confidence and the mere lending of more money to shaky institutions could not stop this downward course. A prompt program applied as quickly as possible seemed to me not only justified but imperative to our national security. The Congress, and when I say Congress I mean the members of both political parties, fully understood this and gave me generous and intelligent support. The members of Congress realized that the methods of normal times had to be replaced in the emergency by measures which were suited to the serious and pressing requirements of the moment. There was no actual surrender of power, Congress still retained its constitutional authority, and no one has the slightest desire to change the balance of these powers. The function of Congress is to decide what has to be done and to select the appropriate agency to carry out its will. To this policy it has strictly adhered. The only thing that has been happening has been to designate the President as the agency to carry out certain of the purposes of the Congress. This was constitutional and in keeping with the past American tradition.

The legislation which has been passed or is in the process of enactment can properly be considered as part of a well-grounded plan.

First, we are giving opportunity of employment to one-quarter of a million of the unemployed, especially the young men who have dependents, to go into the forestry and flood prevention work. This is a big task because it means feeding, clothing and caring for nearly twice as many men as we have in the regular army itself. In creating this civilian conservation corps we are killing two birds with one stone. We are clearly enhancing the value of our natural resources and we are relieving an appreciable amount of actual distress. This great group of men has entered upon its work on a purely voluntary basis; no military training is involved and we are conserving not only our natural resources, but our human resources. One of the great values to this work is the fact that it is direct and requires the intervention of very little machinery.

Second, I have requested the Congress and have secured action upon a proposal to put the great properties owned by our government at Muscle Shoals to work after long years of wasteful inaction, and with this a broad plan for the improvement of a vast area in the Tennessee Valley. It will add to the comfort and happiness of hundreds of thousands of people and the incident benefits will reach the entire nation.

Next, the Congress is about to pass legislation that will greatly ease the mortgage distress among the farmers and the home owners of the nation, by providing for the easing of the burden of debt now bearing so heavily upon millions of our people.

Our next step in seeking immediate relief is a grant of half a billion dollars to help the states, counties and municipalities in their duty to care for those who need direct and immediate relief.

The Congress also passed legislation authorizing the sale of beer in such states as desired it. This has already resulted in considerable reemployment and incidentally has provided much needed tax revenue.

We are planning to ask the Congress for legislation to enable the government to undertake public works, thus stimulating directly and indirectly the employment of many others in well-considered projects.

Further legislation has been taken up which goes much more fundamentally into our economic problems. The Farm Relief Bill seeks by the use of several methods, alone or together, to bring about an increased return to farmers for their major farm products, seeking at the same time to prevent in the days to come disastrous overproduction which so often in the past has kept farm commodity prices far below a reasonable return. This measure provides wide powers for emergencies. The extent of its use will depend entirely upon what the future has in store.

Well-considered and conservative measures will likewise be proposed which will attempt to give to the industrial workers of the country a more fair wage return, prevent cut-throat competition and unduly long hours for labor, and at the same time encourage each industry to prevent overproduction.

Our Railroad Bill falls into the same class because it seeks to provide and make certain definite planning by the railroads themselves, with the assistance of the government, to eliminate the duplication and waste that is now resulting in railroad receiverships and continuing operating deficits.

I am certain that the people of this country understand and approve the broad purposes behind these new governmental policies relating to agriculture and industry and transportation. We found ourselves faced with more agricultural products than we could possibly consume ourselves and surpluses which other nations did not have the cash to buy from us except at prices ruinously low. We found our factories able to turn out more goods than we could possibly consume, and at the same time we were faced with a falling export demand. We found ourselves with more facilities to transport goods and crops than there were goods and crops to be transported. All of this has been caused in large part by a complete lack of planning and a complete failure to understand the danger signals that have been flying ever since the close of the World War. The people of this country have been erroneously encouraged to believe that they could keep on increasing the output of farm and factory indefinitely and that some magician would find ways and means for that increased output to be consumed with reasonable profit to the producer.

Today we have reason to believe that things are a little better than they were two months ago. Industry has picked up, railroads are carrying more freight, farm prices are better, but I am not going to indulge in issuing proclamations of overenthusiastic assurance. We cannot ballyhoo ourselves back to prosperity. I am going to be honest at all times with the people of the country. I do not want the people of this country to take the foolish course of letting this improvement come back on another speculative wave. I do not want the people to believe that because of unjustified optimism we can resume the ruinous practice of increasing our crop output and our factory output in the hope that a kind Providence will find buyers at high prices. Such a course may bring us immediate and false prosperity but it will be the kind of prosperity that will lead us into another tailspin.

It is wholly wrong to call the measure that we have taken government control of farming, control of industry, and control of transportation. It is rather a partnership between government and farming and industry and transportation, not partnership in profits, for the profits still go to the citizens, but rather a partnership in planning and partnership to see that the plans are carried out.

Let me illustrate with an example. Take the cotton goods industry. It is probably true that ninety percent of the cotton manufacturers would agree to eliminate starvation wages, would agree to stop long hours of employment, would agree to stop child labor, would agree to prevent an overproduction that would result in unsalable surpluses. But, what good is such an agreement if the other ten percent of cotton manufacturers pay starvation wages, require long hours, employ children in their mills and turn out burdensome surpluses? The unfair ten percent could produce goods so cheaply that the fair ninety percent would be compelled to meet the unfair conditions. Here is where government comes in. Government ought to have the right and will have the right, after surveying and planning for an industry to prevent, with the assistance of the overwhelming majority of that industry, unfair practice and to enforce this agreement by the authority of government. The so- called anti-trust laws were intended to prevent the creation of monopolies. That purpose of the anti-trust laws must be continued, but these laws were never intended to encourage the kind of unfair competition that results in long hours, starvation wages and overproduction.

The same principle applies to farm products and to transportation and every other field of organized private industry.

We are working toward a definite goal, which is to prevent the return of conditions which came very close to destroying what we call modern civilization. The actual accomplishment of our purpose cannot be attained in a day. Our policies are wholly within purposes for which our American constitutional government was established 150 years ago.

I know that the people of this country will understand this and will also understand the spirit in which we are undertaking this policy. I do not deny that we may make mistakes of procedure as we carry out the policy. I have no expectation of making a hit every time I come to bat. What I seek is the highest possible batting average, not only for myself but for the team. Theodore Roosevelt once said to me: "If I can be right 75 percent of the time I shall come up to the fullest measure of my hopes."

Much has been said of late about federal finances and inflation, the gold standard, etc. Let me make the facts very simple and my policy very clear. In the first place, government credit and government currency are really one and the same thing. Behind government bonds there is only a promise to pay. Behind government currency we have, in addition to the promise to pay, a reserve of gold and a small reserve of silver. In this connection it is worth while remembering that in the past the government has agreed to redeem nearly thirty billions of its debts and its currency in gold, and private corporations in this country have agreed to redeem another sixty or seventy billions of securities and mortgages in gold. The government and private corporations were making these agreements when they knew full well that all of the gold in the United States amounted to only between three and four billions and that all of the gold in all of the world amounted to only about eleven billions.

If the holders of these promises to pay started in to demand gold the first comers would get gold for a few days and they would amount to about one twenty-fifth of the holders of the securities and the currency. The other twenty-four people out of twenty-five, who did not happen to be at the top of the line, would be told politely that there was no more gold left. We have decided to treat all twenty-five in the same way in the interest of justice and the exercise of the constitutional powers of this government. We have placed everyone on the same basis in order that the general good may be preserved.

Nevertheless, gold, and to a partial extent silver, are perfectly good bases for currency and that is why I decided not to let any of the gold now in the country go out of it.

A series of conditions arose three weeks ago which very readily might have meant, first, a drain on our gold by foreign countries, and second, as a result of that, a flight of American capital, in the form of gold, out of our country. It is not exaggerating the possibility to tell you that such an occurrence might well have taken from us the major part of our gold reserve and resulted in such a further weakening of our government and private credit as to bring on actual panic conditions and the complete stoppage of the wheels of industry.

The administration has the definite objective of raising commodity prices to such an extent that those who have borrowed money will, on the average, be able to repay that money in the same kind of dollar which they borrowed. We do not seek to let them get such a cheap dollar that they will be able to pay back a great deal less than they borrowed. In other words, we seek to correct a wrong and not to create another wrong in the opposite direction. That is why powers are being given to the administration to provide, if necessary, for an enlargement of credit, in order to correct the existing wrong. These powers will be used when, as, and if it may be necessary to accomplish the purpose.

Hand in hand with the domestic situation which, of course, is our first concern, is the world situation, and I want to emphasize to you that the domestic situation is inevitably and deeply tied in with the conditions in all of the other nations of the world. In other words, we can get, in all probability, a fair measure of prosperity to return in the United States, but it will not be permanent unless we get a return to prosperity all over the world.

In the conferences which we have held and are holding with the leaders of other nations, we are seeking four great objectives: First, a general reduction of armaments and through this the removal of the fear of invasion and armed attack, and, at the same time, a reduction in armament costs, in order to help in the balancing of government budgets and the reduction of taxation; second, a cutting down of the trade barriers, in order to restart the flow of exchange of crops and goods between nations; third, the setting up of a stabilization of currencies, in order that trade can make contracts ahead; fourth, the reestablishment of friendly relations and greater confidence between all nations.

Our foreign visitors these past three weeks have responded to these purposes in a very helpful way. All of the nations have suffered alike in this great depression. They have all reached the conclusion that each can best be helped by the common action of all. It is in this spirit that our visitors have met with us and discussed our common problems. The international conference that lies before us must succeed. The future of the world demands it and we have each of us pledged ourselves to the best joint efforts to this end.

To you, the people of this country, all of us, the Members of the Congress and the members of this administration, owe a profound debt of gratitude. Throughout the depression you have been patient. You have granted us wide powers; you have encouraged us with a widespread approval of our purposes.

Every ounce of strength and every resource at our command we have devoted to the end of justifying your confidence. We are encouraged to believe that a wise and sensible beginning has been made. In the present spirit of mutual confidence and mutual encouragement we go forward.

July 24, 1933.

After the adjournment of the historical special session of the Congress five weeks ago I purposely refrained from addressing you for two very good reasons.

First, I think that we all wanted the opportunity of a little quiet thought to examine and assimilate in a mental picture the crowding events of the hundred days which had been devoted to the starting of the wheels of the New Deal.

Secondly, I wanted a few weeks in which to set up the new administrative organization and to see the first fruits of our careful planning.

I think it will interest you if I set forth the fundamentals of this planning for national recovery; and this I am very certain will make it abundantly clear to you that all of the proposals and all of the legislation since the fourth day of March have not been just a collection of haphazard schemes but rather the orderly component parts of a connected and logical whole.

Long before inauguration day I became convinced that individual effort and local effort and even disjointed federal effort had failed and of necessity would fail and, therefore, that a rounded leadership by the federal government had become a necessity both of theory and of fact. Such leadership, however, had its beginning in preserving and strengthening the credit of the United States government, because without that no leadership was a possibility. For years the government had not lived within its income. The immediate task was to bring our regular expenses within our revenues. That has been done.

It may seem inconsistent for a government to cut down its regular expenses and at the same time to borrow and to spend billions for an emergency. But it is not inconsistent because a large portion of the emergency money has been paid out in the form of sound loans which will be repaid to the treasury over a period of years; and to cover the rest of the emergency money we have imposed taxes to pay the interest and the installments on that part of the debt.

So you will see that we have kept our credit good. We have built a granite foundation in a period of confusion. That foundation of the federal credit stands there broad and sure. It is the base of the whole recovery plan.

Then came the part of the problem that concerned the credit of the individual citizens themselves. You and I know of the banking crisis and of the great danger to the savings of our people. On March sixth every national bank was closed. One month later 90 percent of the deposits in the national banks had been made available to the depositors. Today only about 5 percent of the deposits in national banks are still tied up. The condition relating to state banks, while not quite so good on a percentage basis, is showing a steady reduction in the total of frozen deposits—a result much better than we had expected three months ago.

The problem of the credit of the individual was made more difficult because of another fact. The dollar was a different dollar from the one with which the average debt had been incurred. For this reason large numbers of people were actually losing possession of and title to their farms and homes. All of you know the financial steps which have been taken to correct this inequality. In addition the Home Loan Act, the Farm Loan Act and the Bankruptcy Act were passed.

It was a vital necessity to restore purchasing power by reducing the debt and interest charges upon our people, but while we were helping people to save their credit it was at the same time absolutely essential to do something about the physical needs of hundreds of thousands who were in dire straits at that very moment. Municipal and state aid were being stretched to the limit. We appropriated half a billion dollars to supplement their efforts and in addition, as you know, we have put 300,000 young men into practical and useful work in our forests and to prevent flood and soil erosion. The wages they earn are going in greater part to the support of the nearly one million people who constitute their families.

In this same classification we can properly place the great public works program running to a total of over three billion dollars—to be used for highways and ships and flood prevention and inland navigation and thousands of self-sustaining state and municipal improvements. Two points should be made clear in the allotting and administration of these projects—first, we are using the utmost care to choose labor-creating, quick-acting, useful projects, avoiding the smell of the pork barrel; and secondly, we are hoping that at least half of the money will come back to the government from projects which will pay for themselves over a period of years.

Thus far I have spoken primarily of the foundation stones—the measures that were necessary to reestablish credit and to head people in the opposite direction by preventing distress and providing as much work as possible through governmental agencies. Now I come to the links which will build us a more lasting prosperity. I have said that we cannot attain that in a nation half boom and half broke. If all of our people have work and fair wages and fair profits, they can buy the products of their neighbors and business is good. But if you take away the wages and the profits of half of them, business is only half as good. It doesn't help much if the fortunate half is very prosperous—the best way is for everybody to be reasonably prosperous.

For many years the two great barriers to a normal prosperity have been low farm prices and the creeping paralysis of unemployment. These factors have cut the purchasing power of the country in half. I promised action. Congress did its part when it passed the Farm and the Industrial Recovery Acts. Today we are putting these two acts to work and they will work if people understand their plain objectives.

First the Farm Act: It is based on the fact that the purchasing power of nearly half our population depends on adequate prices for farm products. We have been producing more of some crops than we consume or can sell in a depressed world market. The cure is not to produce so much. Without our help the farmers cannot get together and cut production, and the Farm Bill gives them a method of bringing their production down to a reasonable level and of obtaining reasonable prices for their crops. I have clearly stated that this method is in a sense experimental, but so far as we have gone we have reason to believe that it will produce good results.

It is obvious that if we can greatly increase the purchasing power of the tens of millions of our people who make a living from farming and the distribution of farm crops, we will greatly increase the consumption of those goods which are turned out by industry.

That brings me to the final step—bringing back industry along sound lines.

Last Autumn, on several occasions, I expressed my faith that we can make possible by democratic self-discipline in industry general increases in wages and shortening of hours sufficient to enable industry to pay its own workers enough to let those workers buy and use the things that their labor produces. This can be done only if we permit and encourage cooperative action in industry because it is obvious that without united action a few selfish men in each competitive group will pay starvation wages and insist on long hours of work. Others in that group must either follow suit or close up shop. We have seen the result of action of that kind in the continuing descent into the economic Hell of the past four years.

There is a clear way to reverse that process: If all employers in each competitive group agree to pay their workers the same wages—reasonable wages—and require the same hours—reasonable hours—then higher wages and shorter hours will hurt no employer. Moreover, such action is better for the employer than unemployment and low wages, because it makes more buyers for his product. That is the simple idea which is the very heart of the Industrial Recovery Act.

On the basis of this simple principle of everybody doing things together, we are starting out on this nationwide attack on unemployment. It will succeed if our people understand it—in the big industries, in the little shops, in the great cities and in the small villages. There is nothing complicated about it and there is nothing particularly new in the principle. It goes back to the basic idea of society and of the nation itself that people acting in a group can accomplish things which no individual acting alone could even hope to bring about.

Here is an example. In the Cotton Textile Code and in other agreements already signed, child labor has been abolished. That makes me personally happier than any other one thing with which I have been connected since I came to Washington. In the textile industry—an industry which came to me spontaneously and with a splendid cooperation as soon as the recovery act was signed—child labor was an old evil. But no employer acting alone was able to wipe it out. If one employer tried it, or if one state tried it, the costs of operation rose so high that it was impossible to compete with the employers or states which had failed to act. The moment the Recovery Act was passed, this monstrous thing which neither opinion nor law could reach through years of effort went out in a flash. As a British editorial put it, we did more under a Code in one day than they in England had been able to do under the common law in eighty-five years of effort. I use this incident, my friends, not to boast of what has already been done but to point the way to you for even greater cooperative efforts this summer and autumn.

We are not going through another winter like the last. I doubt if ever any people so bravely and cheerfully endured a season half so bitter. We cannot ask America to continue to face such needless hardships. It is time for courageous action, and the Recovery Bill gives us the means to conquer unemployment with exactly the same weapon that we have used to strike down child labor.

The proposition is simply this:

If all employers will act together to shorten hours and raise wages we can put people back to work. No employer will suffer, because the relative level of competitive cost will advance by the same amount for all. But if any considerable group should lag or shirk, this great opportunity will pass us by and we will go into another desperate winter. This must not happen.

We have sent out to all employers an agreement which is the result of weeks of consultation. This agreement checks against the voluntary codes of nearly all the large industries which have already been submitted. This blanket agreement carries the unanimous approval of the three boards which I have appointed to advise in this, boards representing the great leaders in labor, in industry and in social service. The agreement has already brought a flood of approval from every state, and from so wide a cross- section of the common calling of industry that I know it is fair for all. It is a plan—deliberate, reasonable and just—intended to put into effect at once the most important of the broad principles which are being established, industry by industry, through codes. Naturally, it takes a good deal of organizing and a great many hearings and many months, to get these codes perfected and signed, and we cannot wait for all of them to go through. The blanket agreements, however, which I am sending to every employer will start the wheels turning now, and not six months from now.

There are, of course, men, a few of them who might thwart this great common purpose by seeking selfish advantage. There are adequate penalties in the law, but I am now asking the cooperation that comes from opinion and from conscience. These are the only instruments we shall use in this great summer offensive against unemployment. But we shall use them to the limit to protect the willing from the laggard and to make the plan succeed.

In war, in the gloom of night attack, soldiers wear a bright badge on their shoulders to be sure that comrades do not fire on comrades. On that principle, those who cooperate in this program must know each other at a glance. That is why we have provided a badge of honor for this purpose, a simple design with a legend. "We do our part," and I ask that all those who join with me shall display that badge prominently. It is essential to our purpose.

Already all the great, basic industries have come forward willingly with proposed codes, and in these codes they accept the principles leading to mass reemployment. But, important as is this heartening demonstration, the richest field for results is among the small employers, those whose contribution will give new work for from one to ten people. These smaller employers are indeed a vital part of the backbone of the country, and the success of our plans lies largely in their hands.

Already the telegrams and letters are pouring into the White House—messages from employers who ask that their names be placed on this special Roll of Honor. They represent great corporations and companies, and partnerships and individuals. I ask that even before the dates set in the agreements which we have sent out, the employers of the country who have not already done so—the big fellows and the little fellows—shall at once write or telegraph to me personally at the White House, expressing their intention of going through with the plan. And it is my purpose to keep posted in the post office of every town, a Roll of Honor of all those who join with me.

I want to take this occasion to say to the twenty-four governors who are now in conference in San Francisco, that nothing thus far has helped in strengthening this great movement more than their resolutions adopted at the very outset of their meeting, giving this plan their unanimous and instant approval, and pledging to support it in their states.

To the men and women whose lives have been darkened by the fact or the fear of unemployment, I am justified in saying a word of encouragement because the codes and the agreements already approved, or about to be passed upon, prove that the plan does raise wages, and that it does put people back to work. You can look on every employer who adopts the plan as one who is doing his part, and those employers deserve well of everyone who works for a living. It will be clear to you, as it is to me, that while the shirking employer may undersell his competitor, the saving he thus makes is made at the expense of his country's welfare.

While we are making this great common effort there should be no discord and dispute. This is no time to cavil or to question the standard set by this universal agreement. It is time for patience and understanding and cooperation. The workers of this country have rights under this law which cannot be taken from them, and nobody will be permitted to whittle them away, but, on the other hand, no aggression is now necessary to attain those rights. The whole country will be united to get them for you. The principle that applies to the employers applies to the workers as well, and I ask you workers to cooperate in the same spirit.

When Andrew Jackson, "Old Hickory," died, someone asked, "Will he go to Heaven?" and the answer was, "He will if he wants to." If I am asked whether the American people will pull themselves out of this depression, I answer, "They will if they want to." The essence of the plan is a universal limitation of hours of work per week for any individual by common consent, and a universal payment of wages above a minimum, also by common consent. I cannot guarantee the success of this nationwide plan, but the people of this country can guarantee its success. I have no faith in "cure-alls" but I believe that we can greatly influence economic forces. I have no sympathy with the professional economists who insist that things must run their course and that human agencies can have no influence on economic ills. One reason is that I happen to know that professional economists have changed their definition of economic laws every five or ten years for a very long time, but I do have faith, and retain faith, in the strength of common purpose, and in the strength of unified action taken by the American people.

That is why I am describing to you the simple purposes and the solid foundations upon which our program of recovery is built. That is why I am asking the employers of the nation to sign this common covenant with me—to sign it in the name of patriotism and humanity. That is why I am asking the workers to go along with us in a spirit of understanding and of helpfulness.

October 22, 1933.

26

It is three months since I have talked with the people of this country about our national problems; but during this period many things have happened, and I am glad to say that the major part of them have greatly helped the well-being of the average citizen.

Because, in every step which your government is taking we are thinking in terms of the average of you—in the old words, "the greatest good to the greatest number"—we, as reasonable people, cannot expect to bring definite benefits to every person or to every occupation or business, or industry or agriculture. In the same way, no reasonable person can expect that in this short space of time, during which new machinery had to be not only put to work, but first set up, that every locality in every one of the forty- eight states of the country could share equally and simultaneously in the trend to better times.

The whole picture, however—the average of the whole territory from coast to coast—the average of the whole population of 120,000,000 people—shows to any person willing to look, facts and action of which you and I can be proud.

In the early spring of this year there were actually and proportionately more people out of work in this country than in any other nation in the world. Fair estimates showed twelve or thirteen millions unemployed last March. Among those there were, of course, several millions who could be classed as normally unemployed—people who worked occasionally when they felt like it, and others who preferred not to work at all. It seems, therefore, fair to say that there were about 10 millions of our citizens who earnestly, and in many cases hungrily, were seeking work and could not get it. Of these, in the short space of a few months, I am convinced that at least 4 millions have been given employment—or, saying it another way, 40 percent of those seeking work have found it.

That does not mean, my friends, that I am satisfied, or that you are satisfied that our work is ended. We have a long way to go but we are on the way.

How are we constructing the edifice of recovery—the temple which, when completed, will no longer be a temple of money-changers or of beggars, but rather a temple dedicated to and maintained for a greater social justice, a greater welfare for America—the habitation of a sound economic life? We are building, stone by stone, the columns which will support that habitation. Those columns are many in number and though, for a moment the progress of one column may disturb the progress on the pillar next to it, the work on all of them must proceed without let or hindrance.

We all know that immediate relief for the unemployed was the first essential of such a structure and that is why I speak first of the fact that three hundred thousand young men have been given employment and are being given employment all through this winter in the Civilian Conservation Corps Camps in almost every part of the nation.

So, too, we have, as you know, expended greater sums in cooperation with states and localities for work relief and home relief than ever before—sums which during the coming winter cannot be lessened for the very simple reason that though several million people have gone back to work, the necessities of those who have not yet obtained work is more severe than at this time last year.

Then we come to the relief that is being given to those who are in danger of losing their farms or their homes. New machinery had to be set up for farm credit and for home credit in every one of the thirty-one hundred counties of the United States, and every day that passes is saving homes and farms to hundreds of families. I have publicly asked that foreclosures on farms and chattels and on homes be delayed until every mortgagor in the country shall have had full opportunity to take advantage of federal credit. I make the further request which many of you know has already been made through the great federal credit organizations that if there is any family in the United States about to lose its home or about to lose its chattels, that family should telegraph at once either to the Farm Credit Administration or the Home Owners Loan Corporation in Washington requesting their help.

Two other great agencies are in full swing. The Reconstruction Finance Corporation continues to lend large sums to industry and finance with the definite objective of making easy the extending of credit to industry, commerce and finance.

The program of public works in three months has advanced to this point: Out of a total appropriated for public works of three billion three hundred million, one billion eight hundred million has already been allocated to federal projects of all kinds and literally in every part of the United States and work on these is starting forward. In addition, three hundred millions have been allocated to public works to be carried out by states, municipalities and private organizations, such as those undertaking slum clearance. The balance of the public works money, nearly all of it intended for state or local projects, waits only on the presentation of proper projects by the states and localities themselves. Washington has the money and is waiting for the proper projects to which to allot it.

Another pillar in the making is the Agricultural Adjustment Administration. I have been amazed by the extraordinary degree of cooperation given to the government by the cotton farmers in the South, the wheat farmers of the West, the tobacco farmers of the Southeast, and I am confident that the corn-hog farmers of the Middle West will come through in the same magnificent fashion. The problem we seek to solve had been steadily getting worse for twenty years, but during the last six months we have made more rapid progress than any nation has ever made in a like period of time. It is true that in July farm commodity prices had been pushed up higher than they are today, but that push came in part from pure speculation by people who could not tell you the difference between wheat and rye, by people who had never seen cotton growing, by people who did not know that hogs were fed on corn—people who have no real interest in the farmer and his problems.

In spite, however, of the speculative reaction from the speculative advance, it seems to be well established that during the course of the year 1933 the farmers of the United States will receive 33 percent more dollars for what they have produced than they received in the year 1932. Put in another way, they will receive $400 in 1933, where they received $300 the year before. That, remember, is for the average of the country, for I have reports that some sections are not any better off than they were a year ago. This applies among the major products, especially to cattle raising and the dairy industry. We are going after those problems as fast as we can.

I do not hesitate to say, in the simplest, clearest language of which I am capable, that although the prices of many products of the farm have gone up and although many farm families are better off than they were last year, I am not satisfied either with the amount or the extent of the rise, and that it is definitely a part of our policy to increase the rise and to extend it to those products which have as yet felt no benefit. If we cannot do this one way we will do it another. Do it, we will.

Standing beside the pillar of the farm—the A.A.A.—is the pillar of industry—the N.R.A. Its object is to put industry and business workers into employment and to increase their purchasing power through increased wages.

It has abolished child labor. It has eliminated the sweat shop. It has ended sixty cents a week paid in some mills and eighty cents a week paid in some mines. The measure of the growth of this pillar lies in the total figures of reemployment which I have already given you and in the fact that reemployment is continuing and not stopping. The secret of N.R.A. is cooperation. That cooperation has been voluntarily given through the signing of the blanket codes and through the signing of specific codes which already include all of the greater industries of the nation.

In the vast majority of cases, in the vast majority of localities—the N.R.A. has been given support in unstinted measure. We know that there are chiselers. At the bottom of every case of criticism and obstruction we have found some selfish interest, some private ax to grind.

Ninety percent of complaints come from misconception. For example, it has been said that N.R.A. has failed to raise the price of wheat and corn and hogs; that N.R.A. has not loaned enough money for local public works. Of course, N.R.A. has nothing whatsoever to do with the price of farm products, nor with public works. It has to do only with industrial organization for economic planning to wipe out unfair practices and to create reemployment. Even in the field of business and industry, N.R.A. does not apply to the rural communities or to towns of under twenty-five hundred population, except in so far as those towns contain factories or chain stores which come under a specific code.

It is also true that among the chiselers to whom I have referred, there are not only the big chiselers but also petty chiselers who seek to make undue profit on untrue statements.

Let me cite to you the example of the salesman in a store in a large Eastern city who tried to justify the increase in the price of a cotton shirt from one dollar and a half to two dollars and a half by saying to the customer that it was due to the cotton processing tax. Actually in that shirt there was about one pound of cotton and the processing tax amounted to four and a quarter cents on that pound of cotton.

At this point it is only fair that I should give credit to the sixty or seventy million people who live in the cities and larger towns of the nation for their understanding and their willingness to go along with the payment of even these small processing taxes, though they know full well that the proportion of the processing taxes on cotton goods and on food products paid for by city dwellers goes 100 percent towards increasing the agricultural income of the farm dwellers of the land.

The last pillar of which I speak is that of the money of the country in the banks of the country. There are two simple facts.

First, the federal government is about to spend one billion dollars as an immediate loan on the frozen or non-liquid assets of all banks closed since January 1, 1933, giving a liberal appraisal to those assets. This money will be in the hands of the depositors as quickly as it is humanly possible to get it out.

Second, the Government Bank Deposit Insurance on all accounts up to $2500 goes into effect on January first. We are now engaged in seeing to it that on or before that date the banking capital structure will be built up by the government to the point that the banks will be in sound condition when the insurance goes into effect.

Finally, I repeat what I have said on many occasions, that ever since last March the definite policy of the government has been to restore commodity price levels. The object has been the attainment of such a level as will enable agriculture and industry once more to give work to the unemployed. It has been to make possible the payment of public and private debts more nearly at the price level at which they were incurred. It has been gradually to restore a balance in the price structure so that farmers may exchange their products for the products of industry on a fairer exchange basis. It has been and is also the purpose to prevent prices from rising beyond the point necessary to attain these ends. The permanent welfare and security of every class of our people ultimately depends on our attainment of these purposes.

Obviously, and because hundreds of different kinds of crops and industrial occupations in the huge territory that makes up this Nation are involved, we cannot reach the goal in only a few months. We may take one year or two years or three years.

No one who considers the plain facts of our situation believes that commodity prices, especially agricultural prices, are high enough yet.

Some people are putting the cart before the horse. They want a permanent revaluation of the dollar first. It is the government's policy to restore the price level first. I would not know, and no one else could tell, just what the permanent valuation of the dollar will be. To guess at a permanent gold valuation now would certainly require later changes caused by later facts.

When we have restored the price level, we shall seek to establish and maintain a dollar which will not change its purchasing and debt paying power during the succeeding generation. I said that in my message to the American delegation in London last July. And I say it now once more.

Because of conditions in this country and because of events beyond our control in other parts of the world, it becomes increasingly important to develop and apply the further measures which may be necessary from time to time to control the gold value of our own dollar at home.

Our dollar is now altogether too greatly influenced by the accidents of international trade, by the internal policies of other nations and by political disturbance in other continents. Therefore the United States must take firmly in its own hands the control of the gold value of our dollar. This is necessary in order to prevent dollar disturbances from swinging us away from our ultimate goal, namely, the continued recovery of our commodity prices.

As a further effective means to this end, I am going to establish a government market for gold in the United States. Therefore, under the clearly defined authority of existing law, I am authorizing the Reconstruction Finance Corporation to buy gold newly mined in the United States at prices to be determined from time to time after consultation with the Secretary of the Treasury and the President. Whenever necessary to the end in view, we shall also buy or sell gold in the world market.

My aim in taking this step is to establish and maintain continuous control.

This is a policy and not an expedient.

It is not to be used merely to offset a temporary fall in prices. We are thus continuing to move towards a managed currency.

You will recall the dire predictions made last spring by those who did not agree with our common policies of raising prices by direct means. What actually happened stood out in sharp contrast with those predictions. Government credit is high, prices have risen in part. Doubtless prophets of evil still exist in our midst. But government credit will be maintained and a sound currency will accompany a rise in the American commodity price level.

I have told you tonight the story of our steady but sure work in building our common recovery. In my promises to you both before and after March 4th, I made two things plain: First, that I pledged no miracles and, second, that I would do my best.

I thank you for your patience and your faith. Our troubles will not be over tomorrow, but we are on our way and we are headed in the right direction.

June 28, 1934.

It has been several months since I have talked with you concerning the problems of government. Since January, those of us in whom you have vested responsibility have been engaged in the fulfillment of plans and policies which had been widely discussed in previous months. It seemed to us our duty not only to make the right path clear but also to tread that path.

As we review the achievements of this session of the Seventy-third Congress, it is made increasingly clear that its task was essentially that of completing and fortifying the work it had begun in March, 1933. That was no easy task, but the Congress was equal to it. It has been well said that while there were a few exceptions, this Congress displayed a greater freedom from mere partisanship than any other peace-time Congress since the administration of President Washington himself. The session was distinguished by the extent and variety of legislation enacted and by the intelligence and good will of debate upon these measures.

I mention only a few of the major enactments. It provided for the readjustment of the debt burden through the corporate and municipal bankruptcy acts and the Farm Relief Act. It lent a hand to industry by encouraging loans to solvent industries unable to secure adequate help from banking institutions. It strengthened the integrity of finance through the regulation of securities exchanges. It provided a rational method of increasing our volume of foreign trade through reciprocal trading agreements. It strengthened our naval forces to conform with the intentions and permission of existing treaty rights. It made further advances towards peace in industry through the Labor Adjustment Act.

It supplemented our agricultural policy through measures widely demanded by farmers themselves and intended to avert price destroying surpluses. It strengthened the hand of the federal government in its attempts to suppress gangster crime. It took definite steps towards a national housing program through an act which I signed today designed to encourage private capital in the rebuilding of the homes of the nation. It created a permanent federal body for the just regulation of all forms of communication, including the telephone, the telegraph and the radio. Finally, and I believe most important, it reorganized, simplified and made more fair and just our monetary system, setting up standards and policies adequate to meet the necessities of modern economic life, doing justice to both gold and silver as the metal bases behind the currency of the United States.

In the consistent development of our previous efforts toward the saving and safeguarding of our national life, I have continued to recognize three related steps. The first was relief, because the primary concern of any government dominated by the humane ideals of democracy is the simple principle that in a land of vast resources no one should be permitted to starve. Relief was and continues to be our first consideration. It calls for large expenditures and will continue in modified form to do so for a long time to come. We may as well recognize that fact. It comes from the paralysis that arose as the after-effect of that unfortunate decade characterized by a mad chase for unearned riches and an unwillingness of leaders in almost every walk of life to look beyond their own schemes and speculations. In our administration of relief we follow two principles: First, that direct giving shall, wherever possible, be supplemented by provision for useful and remunerative work and, second, that where families in their existing surroundings will in all human probability never find an opportunity for full self- maintenance, happiness and enjoyment, we will try to give them a new chance in new surroundings.

The second step was recovery, and it is sufficient for me to ask each and every one of you to compare the situation in agriculture and in industry today with what it was fifteen months ago.

At the same time we have recognized the necessity of reform and reconstruction—reform because much of our trouble today and in the past few years has been due to a lack of understanding of the elementary principles of justice and fairness by those in whom leadership in business and finance was placed—reconstruction because new conditions in our economic life as well as old but neglected conditions had to be corrected.

Substantial gains well known to all of you have justified our course. I could cite statistics to you as unanswerable measures of our national progress—statistics to show the gain in the average weekly pay envelope of workers in the great majority of industries—statistics to show hundreds of thousands reemployed in private industries and other hundreds of thousands given new employment through the expansion of direct and indirect government assistance of many kinds, although, of course, there are those exceptions in professional pursuits whose economic improvement, of necessity, will be delayed. I also could cite statistics to show the great rise in the value of farm products—statistics to prove the demand for consumers' goods, ranging all the way from food and clothing to automobiles, and of late to prove the rise in the demand for durable goods— statistics to cover the great increase in bank deposits and to show the scores of thousands of homes and of farms which have been saved from foreclosure.

But the simplest way for each of you to judge recovery lies in the plain facts of your own individual situation. Are you better off than you were last year? Are your debts less burdensome? Is your bank account more secure? Are your working conditions better? Is your faith in your own individual future more firmly grounded?

Also, let me put to you another simple question: Have you as an individual paid too high a price for these gains? Plausible self- seekers and theoretical die-hards will tell you of the loss of individual liberty. Answer this question also out of the facts of your own life. Have you lost any of your rights or liberty or constitutional freedom of action and choice? Turn to the Bill of Rights of the Constitution, which I have solemnly sworn to maintain and under which your freedom rests secure. Read each provision of that Bill of Rights and ask yourself whether you personally have suffered the impairment of a single jot of these great assurances. I have no question in my mind as to what your answer will be. The record is written in the experiences of your own personal lives.

In other words, it is not the overwhelming majority of the farmers or manufacturers or workers who deny the substantial gains of the past year. The most vociferous of the Doubting Thomases may be divided roughly into two groups: First, those who seek special political privilege and, second, those who seek special financial privilege. About a year ago I used as an illustration the 90 percent of the cotton manufacturers of the United States who wanted to do the right thing by their employees and by the public but were prevented from doing so by the 10 percent who undercut them by unfair practices and un-American standards. It is well for us to remember that humanity is a long way from being perfect and that a selfish minority in every walk of life—farming, business, finance and even government service itself—will always continue to think of themselves first and their fellow-beings second.

In the working out of a great national program which seeks the primary good of the greater number, it is true that the toes of some people are being stepped on and are going to be stepped on. But these toes belong to the comparative few who seek to retain or to gain position or riches or both by some short cut which is harmful to the greater good.

In the execution of the powers conferred on it by Congress, the administration needs and will tirelessly seek the best ability that the country affords. Public service offers better rewards in the opportunity for service than ever before in our history—not great salaries, but enough to live on. In the building of this service there are coming to us men and women with ability and courage from every part of the Union. The days of the seeking of mere party advantage through the misuse of public power are drawing to a close. We are increasingly demanding and getting devotion to the public service on the part of every member of the administration, high and low.

The program of the past year is definitely in operation and that operation month by month is being made to fit into the web of old and new conditions. This process of evolution is well illustrated by the constant changes in detailed organization and method going on in the National Recovery Administration. With every passing month we are making strides in the orderly handling of the relationship between employees and employers. Conditions differ, of course, in almost every part of the country and in almost every industry. Temporary methods of adjustment are being replaced by more permanent machinery and, I am glad to say, by a growing recognition on the part of employers and employees of the desirability of maintaining fair relationships all around.

So also, while almost everybody has recognized the tremendous strides in the elimination of child labor, in the payment of not less than fair minimum wages and in the shortening of hours, we are still feeling our way in solving problems which relate to self- government in industry, especially where such self-government tends to eliminate the fair operation of competition.

In this same process of evolution we are keeping before us the objectives of protecting on the one hand industry against chiselers within its own ranks, and on the other hand the consumer through the maintenance of reasonable competition for the prevention of the unfair sky-rocketing of retail prices.

But, in addition to this our immediate task, we must still look to the larger future. I have pointed out to the Congress that we are seeking to find the way once more to well-known, long-established but to some degree forgotten ideals and values. We seek the security of the men, women and children of the nation.

That security involves added means of providing better homes for the people of the nation. That is the first principle of our future program.

The second is to plan the use of land and water resources of this country to the end that the means of livelihood of our citizens may be more adequate to meet their daily needs.

And, finally, the third principle is to use the agencies of government to assist in the establishment of means to provide sound and adequate protection against the vicissitudes of modern life—in other words, social insurance.

Later in the year I hope to talk with you more fully about these plans.

A few timid people, who fear progress, will try to give you new and strange names for what we are doing. Sometimes they will call it "Fascism", sometimes "Communism", sometimes "Regimentation", sometimes "Socialism". But, in so doing, they are trying to make very complex and theoretical something that is really very simple and very practical.

I believe in practical explanations and in practical policies. I believe that what we are doing today is a necessary fulfillment of what Americans have always been doing—a fulfillment of old and tested American ideals.

Let me give you a simple illustration:

While I am away from Washington this summer, a long needed renovation of and addition to our White House office building is to be started. The architects have planned a few new rooms built into the present all too small one-story structure. We are going to include in this addition and in this renovation modern electric wiring and modern plumbing and modern means of keeping the offices cool in the hot Washington summers. But the structural lines of the old Executive Office Building will remain. The artistic lines of the White House buildings were the creation of master builders when our Republic was young. The simplicity and the strength of the structure remain in the face of every modern test. But within this magnificent pattern, the necessities of modern government business require constant reorganization and rebuilding.

If I were to listen to the arguments of some prophets of calamity who are talking these days, I should hesitate to make these alterations. I should fear that while I am away for a few weeks the architects might build some strange new Gothic tower or a factory building or perhaps a replica of the Kremlin or of the Potsdam Palace. But I have no such fears. The architects and builders are men of common sense and of artistic American tastes. They know that the principles of harmony and of necessity itself require that the building of the new structure shall blend with the essential lines of the old. It is this combination of the old and the new that marks orderly peaceful progress—not only in building buildings but in building government itself.

Our new structure is a part of and a fulfillment of the old.

All that we do seeks to fulfill the historic traditions of the American people. Other nations may sacrifice democracy for the transitory stimulation of old and discredited autocracies. We are restoring confidence and well-being under the rule of the people themselves. We remain, as John Marshall said a century ago, "emphatically and truly, a government of the people." Our government "in form and in substance . . . emanates from them. Its powers are granted by them, and are to be exercised directly on them, and for their benefits."

Before I close, I want to tell you of the interest and pleasure with which I look forward to the trip on which I hope to start in a few days. It is a good thing for everyone who can possibly do so to get away at least once a year for a change of scene. I do not want to get into the position of not being able to see the forest because of the thickness of the trees.

I hope to visit our fellow Americans in Puerto Rico, in the Virgin Islands, in the Canal Zone and in Hawaii. And, incidentally, it will give me an opportunity to exchange a friendly word of greeting to the Presidents of our sister Republics: Haiti, Colombia and Panama.

After four weeks on board ship, I plan to land at a port in our Pacific northwest, and then will come the best part of the whole trip, for I am hoping to inspect a number of our new great national projects on the Columbia, Missouri and Mississippi Rivers, to see some of our national parks and, incidentally, to learn much of actual conditions during the trip across the continent back to Washington.

While I was in France during the War our boys used to call the United States "God's country". Let us make it and keep it "God's country".

September 30, 1934.

Three months have passed since I talked with you shortly after the adjournment of the Congress. Tonight I continue that report, though, because of the shortness of time, I must defer a number of subjects to a later date.

Recently the most notable public questions that have concerned us all have had to do with industry and labor and with respect to these, certain developments have taken place which I consider of importance. I am happy to report that after years of uncertainty, culminating in the collapse of the spring of 1933, we are bringing order out of the old chaos with a greater certainty of the employment of labor at a reasonable wage and of more business at a fair profit. These governmental and industrial developments hold promise of new achievements for the nation.

Men may differ as to the particular form of governmental activity with respect to industry and business, but nearly all are agreed that private enterprise in times such as these cannot be left without assistance and without reasonable safeguards lest it destroy not only itself but also our processes of civilization. The underlying necessity for such activity is indeed as strong now as it was years ago when Elihu Root said the following very significant words:

"Instead of the give and take of free individual contract, the tremendous power of organization has combined great aggregations of capital in enormous industrial establishments working through vast agencies of commerce and employing great masses of men in movements of production and transportation and trade, so great in the mass that each individual concerned in them is quite helpless by himself. The relations between the employer and the employed, between the owners of aggregated capital and the units of organized labor, between the small producer, the small trader, the consumer, and the great transporting and manufacturing and distributing agencies, all present new questions for the solution of which the old reliance upon the free action of individual wills appears quite inadequate. And in many directions, the intervention of that organized control which we call government seems necessary to produce the same result of justice and right conduct which obtained through the attrition of individuals before the new conditions arose."

It was in this spirit thus described by Secretary Root that we approached our task of reviving private enterprise in March, 1933. Our first problem was, of course, the banking situation because, as you know, the banks had collapsed. Some banks could not be saved but the great majority of them, either through their own resources or with government aid, have been restored to complete public confidence. This has given safety to millions of depositors in these banks. Closely following this great constructive effort we have, through various federal agencies, saved debtors and creditors alike in many other fields of enterprise, such as loans on farm mortgages and home mortgages; loans to the railroads and insurance companies and, finally, help for home owners and industry itself.

In all of these efforts the government has come to the assistance of business and with the full expectation that the money used to assist these enterprises will eventually be repaid. I believe it will be.

The second step we have taken in the restoration of normal business enterprise has been to clean up thoroughly unwholesome conditions in the field of investment. In this we have had assistance from many bankers and businessmen, most of whom recognize the past evils in the banking system, in the sale of securities, in the deliberate encouragement of stock gambling, in the sale of unsound mortgages and in many other ways in which the public lost billions of dollars. They saw that without changes in the policies and methods of investment there could be no recovery of public confidence in the security of savings. The country now enjoys the safety of bank savings under the new banking laws, the careful checking of new securities under the Securities Act and the curtailment of rank stock speculation through the Securities Exchange Act. I sincerely hope that as a result people will be discouraged in unhappy efforts to get rich quick by speculating in securities. The average person almost always loses. Only a very small minority of the people of this country believe in gambling as a substitute for the old philosophy of Benjamin Franklin that the way to wealth is through work.

In meeting the problems of industrial recovery the chief agency of the government has been the National Recovery Administration. Under its guidance, trades and industries covering over 90 percent of all industrial employees have adopted codes of fair competition, which have been approved by the President. Under these codes, in the industries covered, child labor has been eliminated. The work day and the work week have been shortened. Minimum wages have been established and other wages adjusted toward a rising standard of living. The emergency purpose of the N.R.A. was to put men to work and since its creation more than four million persons have been reemployed, in great part through the cooperation of American business brought about under the codes.

Benefits of the Industrial Recovery Program have come, not only to labor in the form of new jobs, in relief from overwork and in relief from underpay, but also to the owners and managers of industry because, together with a great increase in the payrolls, there has come a substantial rise in the total of industrial profits—a rise from a deficit figure in the first quarter of 1933 to a level of sustained profits within one year from the inauguration of N.R.A.

Now it should not be expected that even employed labor and capital would be completely satisfied with present conditions. Employed workers have not by any means all enjoyed a return to the earnings of prosperous times, although millions of hitherto underprivileged workers are today far better paid than ever before. Also, billions of dollars of invested capital have today a greater security of present and future earning power than before. This is because of the establishment of fair, competitive standards and because of relief from unfair competition in wage cutting which depresses markets and destroys purchasing power. But it is an undeniable fact that the restoration of other billions of sound investments to a reasonable earning power could not be brought about in one year. There is no magic formula, no economic panacea, which could simply revive over-night the heavy industries and the trades dependent upon them.

Nevertheless the gains of trade and industry, as a whole, have been substantial. In these gains and in the policies of the administration there are assurances that hearten all forward- looking men and women with the confidence that we are definitely rebuilding our political and economic system on the lines laid down by the New Deal—lines which as I have so often made clear, are in complete accord with the underlying principles of orderly popular government which Americans have demanded since the white man first came to these shores. We count, in the future as in the past, on the driving power of individual initiative and the incentive of fair private profit, strengthened with the acceptance of those obligations to the public interest which rest upon us all. We have the right to expect that this driving power will be given patriotically and whole-heartedly to our nation.

We have passed through the formative period of code making in the National Recovery Administration and have effected a reorganization of the N.R.A. suited to the needs of the next phase, which is, in turn, a period of preparation for legislation which will determine its permanent form.

In this recent reorganization we have recognized three distinct functions: first, the legislative or policy making function; second, the administrative function of code making and revision; and, third, the judicial function, which includes enforcement, consumer complaints and the settlement of disputes between employers and employees and between one employer and another.

We are now prepared to move into this second phase, on the basis of our experience in the first phase under the able and energetic leadership of General Johnson.

We shall watch carefully the working of this new machinery for the second phase of N.R.A., modifying it where it needs modification and finally making recommendations to the Congress, in order that the functions of N.R.A. which have proved their worth may be made a part of the permanent machinery of government.

Let me call your attention to the fact that the national Industrial Recovery Act gave businessmen the opportunity they had sought for years to improve business conditions through what has been called self-government in industry. If the codes which have been written have been too complicated, if they have gone too far in such matters as price fixing and limitation of production, let it be remembered that so far as possible, consistent with the immediate public interest of this past year and the vital necessity of improving labor conditions, the representatives of trade and industry were permitted to write their ideas into the codes. It is now time to review these actions as a whole to determine through deliberative means in the light of experience, from the standpoint of the good of the industries themselves, as well as the general public interest, whether the methods and policies adopted in the emergency have been best calculated to promote industrial recovery and a permanent improvement of business and labor conditions. There may be a serious question as to the wisdom of many of those devices to control production, or to prevent destructive price cutting which many business organizations have insisted were necessary, or whether their effect may have been to prevent that volume of production which would make possible lower prices and increased employment. Another question arises as to whether in fixing minimum wages on the basis of an hourly or weekly wage we have reached into the heart of the problem which is to provide such annual earnings for the lowest paid worker as will meet his minimum needs. We also question the wisdom of extending code requirements suited to the great industrial centers and to large employers, to the great number of small employers in the smaller communities.

During the last twelve months our industrial recovery has been to some extent retarded by strikes, including a few of major importance. I would not minimize the inevitable losses to employers and employees and to the general public through such conflicts. But I would point out that the extent and severity of labor disputes during this period has been far less than in any previous, comparable period.

When the businessmen of the country were demanding the right to organize themselves adequately to promote their legitimate interests; when the farmers were demanding legislation which would give them opportunities and incentives to organize themselves for a common advance, it was natural that the workers should seek and obtain a statutory declaration of their constitutional right to organize themselves for collective bargaining as embodied in Section 7 (a) of the national Industrial Recovery Act.

Machinery set up by the federal government has provided some new methods of adjustment. Both employers and employees must share the blame of not using them as fully as they should. The employer who turns away from impartial agencies of peace, who denies freedom of organization to his employees, or fails to make every reasonable effort at a peaceful solution of their differences, is not fully supporting the recovery effort of his government. The workers who turn away from these same impartial agencies and decline to use their good offices to gain their ends are likewise not fully cooperating with their government.

It is time that we made a clean-cut effort to bring about that united action of management and labor, which is one of the high purposes of the Recovery Act. We have passed through more than a year of education. Step by step we have created all the government agencies necessary to insure, as a general rule, industrial peace, with justice for all those willing to use these agencies whenever their voluntary bargaining fails to produce a necessary agreement.

There should be at least a full and fair trial given to these means of ending industrial warfare; and in such an effort we should be able to secure for employers and employees and consumers the benefits that all derive from the continuous, peaceful operation of our essential enterprises.

Accordingly, I propose to confer within the coming month with small groups of those truly representative of large employers of labor and of large groups of organized labor, in order to seek their cooperation in establishing what I may describe as a specific trial period of industrial peace.

From those willing to join in establishing this hoped-for period of peace, I shall seek assurances of the making and maintenance of agreements, which can be mutually relied upon, under which wages, hours and working conditions may be determined and any later adjustments shall be made either by agreement or, in case of disagreement, through the mediation or arbitration of state or federal agencies. I shall not ask either employers or employees permanently to lay aside the weapons common to industrial war. But I shall ask both groups to give a fair trial to peaceful methods of adjusting their conflicts of opinion and interest, and to experiment for a reasonable time with measures suitable to civilize our industrial civilization.

Closely allied to the N.R.A. is the program of Public Works provided for in the same Act and designed to put more men back to work, both directly on the public works themselves, and indirectly in the industries supplying the materials for these public works. To those who say that our expenditures for public works and other means for recovery are a waste that we cannot afford, I answer that no country, however rich, can afford the waste of its human resources. Demoralization caused by vast unemployment is our greatest extravagance. Morally, it is the greatest menace to our social order. Some people try to tell me that we must make up our minds that for the future we shall permanently have millions of unemployed just as other countries have had them for over a decade. What may be necessary for those countries is not my responsibility to determine. But as for this country, I stand or fall by my refusal to accept as a necessary condition of our future a permanent army of unemployed. On the contrary, we must make it a national principle that we will not tolerate a large army of unemployed and that we will arrange our national economy to end our present unemployment as soon as we can and then to take wise measures against its return. I do not want to think that it is the destiny of any American to remain permanently on relief rolls.

Those, fortunately few in number, who are frightened by boldness and cowed by the necessity for making decisions, complain that all we have done is unnecessary and subject to great risks. Now that these people are coming out of their storm cellars, they forget that there ever was a storm. They point to England. They would have you believe that England has made progress out of her depression by a do-nothing policy, by letting nature take her course. England has her peculiarities and we have ours but I do not believe any intelligent observer can accuse England of undue orthodoxy in the present emergency.

Did England let nature take her course? No. Did England hold to the gold standard when her reserves were threatened? No. Has England gone back to the gold standard today? No. Did England hesitate to call in ten billion dollars of her war bonds bearing 5 percent interest, to issue new bonds therefore bearing only 3-1/2 percent interest, thereby saving the British treasury one hundred and fifty million dollars a year in interest alone? No. And let it be recorded that the British bankers helped. Is it not a fact that ever since the year 1909, Great Britain in many ways has advanced further along lines of social security than the United States? Is it not a fact that relations between capital and labor on the basis of collective bargaining are much further advanced in Great Britain than in the United States? It is perhaps not strange that the conservative British press has told us with pardonable irony that much of our New Deal program is only an attempt to catch up with English reforms that go back ten years or more.

Nearly all Americans are sensible and calm people. We do not get greatly excited nor is our peace of mind disturbed, whether we be businessmen or workers or farmers, by awesome pronouncements concerning the unconstitutionality of some of our measures of recovery and relief and reform. We are not frightened by reactionary lawyers or political editors. All of these cries have been heard before. More than twenty years ago, when Theodore Roosevelt and Woodrow Wilson were attempting to correct abuses in our national life, the great Chief Justice White said:

"There is great danger it seems to me to arise from the constant habit which prevails where anything is opposed or objected to, of referring without rhyme or reason to the Constitution as a means of preventing its accomplishment, thus creating the general impression that the Constitution is but a barrier to progress instead of being the broad highway through which alone true progress may be enjoyed."

In our efforts for recovery we have avoided on the one hand the theory that business should and must be taken over into an all-embracing government. We have avoided on the other hand the equally untenable theory that it is an interference with liberty to offer reasonable help when private enterprise is in need of help. The course we have followed fits the American practice of government—a practice of taking action step by step, of regulating only to meet concrete needs—a practice of courageous recognition of change. I believe with Abraham Lincoln, that "The legitimate object of government is to do for a community of people whatever they need to have done but cannot do at all or cannot do so well for themselves in their separate and individual capacities."

I am not for a return to that definition of liberty under which for many years a free people were being gradually regimented into the service of the privileged few. I prefer and I am sure you prefer that broader definition of liberty under which we are moving forward to greater freedom, to greater security for the average man than he has ever known before in the history of America.

April 28, 1935.

Since my annual message to the Congress on January fourth, last, I have not addressed the general public over the air. In the many weeks since that time the Congress has devoted itself to the arduous task of formulating legislation necessary to the country's welfare. It has made and is making distinct progress.

Before I come to any of the specific measures, however, I want to leave in your minds one clear fact. The administration and the Congress are not proceeding in any haphazard fashion in this task of government. Each of our steps has a definite relationship to every other step. The job of creating a program for the nation's welfare is, in some respects, like the building of a ship. At different points on the coast where I often visit they build great seagoing ships. When one of these ships is under construction and the steel frames have been set in the keel, it is difficult for a person who does not know ships to tell how it will finally look when it is sailing the high seas.

It may seem confused to some, but out of the multitude of detailed parts that go into the making of the structure the creation of a useful instrument for man ultimately comes. It is that way with the making of a national policy. The objective of the nation has greatly changed in three years. Before that time individual self- interest and group selfishness were paramount in public thinking. The general good was at a discount.

Three years of hard thinking have changed the picture. More and more people, because of clearer thinking and a better understanding, are considering the whole rather than a mere part relating to one section or to one crop, or to one industry, or to an individual private occupation. That is a tremendous gain for the principles of democracy. The overwhelming majority of people in this country know how to sift the wheat from the chaff in what they hear and what they read. They know that the process of the constructive rebuilding of America cannot be done in a day or a year, but that it is being done in spite of the few who seek to confuse them and to profit by their confusion. Americans as a whole are feeling a lot better—a lot more cheerful than for many, many years.

The most difficult place in the world to get a clear open perspective of the country as a whole is Washington. I am reminded sometimes of what President Wilson once said: "So many people come to Washington who know things that are not so, and so few people who know anything about what the people of the United States are thinking about." That is why I occasionally leave this scene of action for a few days to go fishing or back home to Hyde Park, so that I can have a chance to think quietly about the country as a whole. "To get away from the trees", as they say, "and to look at the whole forest." This duty of seeing the country in a long-range perspective is one which, in a very special manner, attaches to this office to which you have chosen me. Did you ever stop to think that there are, after all, only two positions in the nation that are filled by the vote of all of the voters—the President and the Vice-President? That makes it particularly necessary for the Vice- President and for me to conceive of our duty toward the entire country. I speak, therefore, tonight, to and of the American people as a whole.

My most immediate concern is in carrying out the purposes of the great work program just enacted by the Congress. Its first objective is to put men and women now on the relief rolls to work and, incidentally, to assist materially in our already unmistakable march toward recovery. I shall not confuse my discussion by a multitude of figures. So many figures are quoted to prove so many things. Sometimes it depends upon what paper you read and what broadcast you hear. Therefore, let us keep our minds on two or three simple, essential facts in connection with this problem of unemployment. It is true that while business and industry are definitely better our relief rolls are still too large. However, for the first time in five years the relief rolls have declined instead of increased during the winter months. They are still declining. The simple fact is that many million more people have private work today than two years ago today or one year ago today, and every day that passes offers more chances to work for those who want to work. In spite of the fact that unemployment remains a serious problem here as in every other nation, we have come to recognize the possibility and the necessity of certain helpful remedial measures. These measures are of two kinds. The first is to make provisions intended to relieve, to minimize, and to prevent future unemployment; the second is to establish the practical means to help those who are unemployed in this present emergency. Our social security legislation is an attempt to answer the first of these questions; our Works Relief program, the second.

The program for social security now pending before the Congress is a necessary part of the future unemployment policy of the government. While our present and projected expenditures for work relief are wholly within the reasonable limits of our national credit resources, it is obvious that we cannot continue to create governmental deficits for that purpose year after year. We must begin now to make provision for the future. That is why our social security program is an important part of the complete picture. It proposes, by means of old age pensions, to help those who have reached the age of retirement to give up their jobs and thus give to the younger generation greater opportunities for work and to give to all a feeling of security as they look toward old age.

The unemployment insurance part of the legislation will not only help to guard the individual in future periods of lay-off against dependence upon relief, but it will, by sustaining purchasing power, cushion the shock of economic distress. Another helpful feature of unemployment insurance is the incentive it will give to employers to plan more carefully in order that unemployment may be prevented by the stabilizing of employment itself.

Provisions for social security, however, are protections for the future. Our responsibility for the immediate necessities of the unemployed has been met by the Congress through the most comprehensive work plan in the history of the nation. Our problem is to put to work three and one-half million employable persons now on the relief rolls. It is a problem quite as much for private industry as for the government.

We are losing no time getting the government's vast work relief program underway, and we have every reason to believe that it should be in full swing by autumn. In directing it, I shall recognize six fundamental principles:

(1)   The projects should be useful.

(2)   Projects shall be of a nature that a considerable proportion of the money spent will go into wages for labor.

(3)   Projects will be sought which promise ultimate return to the federal treasury of a considerable proportion of the costs.

(4)   Funds allotted for each project should be actually and promptly spent and not held over until later years.

(5)   In all cases projects must be of a character to give employment to those on the relief rolls.

(6)   Projects will be allocated to localities or relief areas in relation to the number of workers on relief rolls in those areas.

I next want to make it clear exactly how we shall direct the work.

(1)   I have set up a Division of Applications and Information to which all proposals for the expenditure of money must go for preliminary study and consideration.

(2)   After the Division of Applications and Information has sifted those projects, they will be sent to an Allotment Division composed of representatives of the more important governmental agencies charged with carrying on work relief projects. The group will also include representatives of cities, and of labor, farming, banking and industry. This Allotment Division will consider all of the recommendations submitted to it and such projects as they approve will be next submitted to the President who under the Act is required to make final allocations.

(3) The next step will be to notify the proper government agency in whose field the project falls, and also to notify another agency which I am creating—a Progress Division. This Division will have the duty of coordinating the purchases of materials and supplies and of making certain that people who are employed will be taken from the relief rolls. It will also have the responsibility of determining work payments in various localities, of making full use of existing employment services and to assist people engaged in relief work to move as rapidly as possible back into private employment when such employment is available. Moreover, this Division will be charged with keeping projects moving on schedule.

(4) I have felt it to be essentially wise and prudent to avoid, so far as possible, the creation of new governmental machinery for supervising this work. The national government now has at least sixty different agencies with the staff and the experience and the competence necessary to carry on the two hundred and fifty or three hundred kinds of work that will be undertaken. These agencies, therefore, will simply be doing on a somewhat enlarged scale the same sort of things that they have been doing. This will make certain that the largest possible portion of the funds allotted will be spent for actually creating new work and not for building up expensive overhead organizations here in Washington.

For many months preparations have been under way. The allotment of funds for desirable projects has already begun. The key men for the major responsibilities of this great task already have been selected. I well realize that the country is expecting before this year is out to see the "dirt fly", as they say, in carrying on the work, and I assure my fellow citizens that no energy will be spared in using these funds effectively to make a major attack upon the problem of unemployment.

Our responsibility is to all of the people in this country. This is a great national crusade to destroy enforced idleness which is an enemy of the human spirit generated by this depression. Our attack upon these enemies must be without stint and without discrimination. No sectional, no political distinctions can be permitted.

It must, however, be recognized that when an enterprise of this character is extended over more than three thousand counties throughout the nation, there may be occasional instances of inefficiency, bad management, or misuse of funds. When cases of this kind occur, there will be those, of course, who will try to tell you that the exceptional failure is characteristic of the entire endeavor. It should be remembered that in every big job there are some imperfections. There are chiselers in every walk of life; there are those in every industry who are guilty of unfair practices; every profession has its black sheep, but long experience in government has taught me that the exceptional instances of wrong-doing in government are probably less numerous than in almost every other line of endeavor. The most effective means of preventing such evils in this Works Relief program will be the eternal vigilance of the American people themselves. I call upon my fellow citizens everywhere to cooperate with me in making this the most efficient and the cleanest example of public enterprise the world has ever seen.

It is time to provide a smashing answer for those cynical men who say that a democracy cannot be honest and efficient. If you will help, this can be done. I, therefore, hope you will watch the work in every corner of this Nation. Feel free to criticize. Tell me of instances where work can be done better, or where improper practices prevail. Neither you nor I want criticism conceived in a purely fault-finding or partisan spirit, but I am jealous of the right of every citizen to call to the attention of his or her government examples of how the public money can be more effectively spent for the benefit of the American people.

I now come, my friends, to a part of the remaining business before the Congress. It has under consideration many measures which provide for the rounding out of the program of economic and social reconstruction with which we have been concerned for two years. I can mention only a few of them tonight, but I do not want my mention of specific measures to be interpreted as lack of interest in or disapproval of many other important proposals that are pending.

The National Industrial Recovery Act expires on the sixteenth of June. After careful consideration, I have asked the Congress to extend the life of this useful agency of government. As we have proceeded with the administration of this Act, we have found from time to time more and more useful ways of promoting its purposes. No reasonable person wants to abandon our present gains—we must continue to protect children, to enforce minimum wages, to prevent excessive hours, to safeguard, define and enforce collective bargaining, and, while retaining fair competition, to eliminate so far as humanly possible, the kinds of unfair practices by selfish minorities which unfortunately did more than anything else to bring about the recent collapse of industries.

There is likewise pending before the Congress legislation to provide for the elimination of unnecessary holding companies in the public utility field.

I consider this legislation a positive recovery measure. Power production in this country is virtually back to the 1929 peak. The operating companies in the gas and electric utility field are by and large in good condition. But under holding company domination the utility industry has long been hopelessly at war within itself and with public sentiment. By far the greater part of the general decline in utility securities had occurred before I was inaugurated. The absentee management of unnecessary holding company control has lost touch with, and has lost the sympathy of, the communities it pretends to serve. Even more significantly it has given the country as a whole an uneasy apprehension of overconcentrated economic power.

A business that loses the confidence of its customers and the good-will of the public cannot long continue to be a good risk for the investor. This legislation will serve the investor by ending the conditions which have caused that lack of confidence and good-will. It will put the public utility operating industry on a sound basis for the future, both in its public relations and in its internal relations.

This legislation will not only in the long run result in providing lower electric and gas rates to the consumer, but it will protect the actual value and earning power of properties now owned by thousands of investors who have little protection under the old laws against what used to be called frenzied finance. It will not destroy values.

Not only business recovery, but the general economic recovery of the nation will be greatly stimulated by the enactment of legislation designed to improve the status of our transportation agencies. There is need for legislation providing for the regulation of interstate transportation by buses and trucks, for the regulation of transportation by water, for the strengthening of our Merchant Marine and Air Transport, for the strengthening of the Interstate Commerce Commission to enable it to carry out a rounded conception of the national transportation system in which the benefits of private ownership are retained while the public stake in these important services is protected by the public's government.

Finally, the reestablishment of public confidence in the banks of the nation is one of the most hopeful results of our efforts as a Nation to reestablish public confidence in private banking. We all know that private banking actually exists by virtue of the permission of and regulation by the people as a whole, speaking through their government. Wise public policy, however, requires not only that banking be safe but that its resources be most fully utilized in the economic life of the country. To this end it was decided more than twenty years ago that the government should assume the responsibility of providing a means by which the credit of the nation might be controlled, not by a few private banking institutions, but by a body with public prestige and authority. The answer to this demand was the Federal Reserve System. Twenty years of experience with this system have justified the efforts made to create it, but these twenty years have shown by experience definite possibilities for improvement. Certain proposals made to amend the Federal Reserve Act deserve prompt and favorable action by the Congress. They are a minimum of wise readjustments of our Federal Reserve System in the light of past experience and present needs.

These measures I have mentioned are, in large part, the program which under my constitutional duty I have recommended to the Congress. They are essential factors in a rounded program for national recovery. They contemplate the enrichment of our national life by a sound and rational ordering of its various elements and wise provisions for the protection of the weak against the strong.

Never since my inauguration in March, 1933, have I felt so unmistakably the atmosphere of recovery. But it is more than the recovery of the material basis of our individual lives. It is the recovery of confidence in our democratic processes and institutions. We have survived all of the arduous burdens and the threatening dangers of a great economic calamity. We have in the darkest moments of our national trials retained our faith in our own ability to master our destiny. Fear is vanishing and confidence is growing on every side, renewed faith in the vast possibilities of human beings to improve their material and spiritual status through the instrumentality of the democratic form of government. That faith is receiving its just reward. For that we can be thankful to the God who watches over America.

September 6, 1936.

I have been on a journey of husbandry. I went primarily to see at first hand conditions in the drought states; to see how effectively federal and local authorities are taking care of pressing problems of relief and also how they are to work together to defend the people of this country against the effects of future droughts.

I saw drought devastation in nine states.

I talked with families who had lost their wheat crop, lost their corn crop, lost their livestock, lost the water in their well, lost their garden and come through to the end of the summer without one dollar of cash resources, facing a winter without feed or food—facing a planting season without seed to put in the ground.

That was the extreme case, but there are thousands and thousands of families on Western farms who share the same difficulties.

I saw cattlemen who because of lack of grass or lack of winter feed have been completely compelled to sell all but their breeding stock and will need help to carry even these through the coming winter. I saw livestock kept alive only because water had been brought to them long distances in tank cars. I saw other farm families who have not lost everything but who, because they have made only partial crops, must have some form of help if they are to continue farming next spring.

I shall never forget the fields of wheat so blasted by heat that they cannot be harvested. I shall never forget field after field of corn stunted, earless and stripped of leaves, for what the sun left the grasshoppers took. I saw brown pastures which would not keep a cow on fifty acres.

Yet I would not have you think for a single minute that there is permanent disaster in these drought regions, or that the picture I saw meant depopulating these areas. No cracked earth, no blistering sun, no burning wind, no grasshoppers, are a permanent match for the indomitable American farmers and stockmen and their wives and children who have carried on through desperate days, and inspire us with their self-reliance, their tenacity and their courage. It was their fathers' task to make homes; it is their task to keep those homes; it is our task to help them win their fight.

First let me talk for a minute about this autumn and the coming winter. We have the option, in the case of families who need actual subsistence, of putting them on the dole or putting them to work. They do not want to go on the dole and they are one thousand percent right. We agree, therefore, that we must put them to work for a decent wage; and when we reach that decision we kill two birds with one stone, because these families will earn enough by working, not only to subsist themselves, but to buy food for their stock, and seed for next year's planting. Into this scheme of things there fit of course the government lending agencies which next year, as in the past, will help with production loans.

Every governor with whom I have talked is in full accord with this program of doing work for these farm families, just as every governor agrees that the individual states will take care of their unemployables but that the cost of employing those who are entirely able and willing to work must be borne by the federal government.

If then we know, as we do today, the approximate number of farm families who will require some form of work relief from now on through the winter, we face the question of what kind of work they should do. Let me make it clear that this is not a new question because it has already been answered to a greater or less extent in every one of the drought communities. Beginning in 1934, when we also had serious drought conditions, the state and federal governments cooperated in planning a large number of projects—many of them directly aimed at the alleviation of future drought conditions. In accordance with that program literally thousands of ponds or small reservoirs have been built in order to supply water for stock and to lift the level of the underground water to protect wells from going dry. Thousands of wells have been drilled or deepened; community lakes have been created and irrigation projects are being pushed.

Water conservation by means such as these is being expanded as a result of this new drought all through the Great Plains area, the Western corn belt and in the states that lie further south. In the Middle West water conservation is not so pressing a problem. Here the work projects run more to soil erosion control and the building of farm-to-market roads.

Spending like this is not waste. It would spell future waste if we did not spend for such things now. These emergency work projects provide money to buy food and clothing for the winter; they keep the livestock on the farm; they provide seed for a new crop, and, best of all, they will conserve soil and water in the future in those areas most frequently hit by drought.

If, for example, in some local area the water table continues to drop and the topsoil to blow away, the land values will disappear with the water and the soil. People on the farms will drift into the nearby cities; the cities will have no farm trade and the workers in the city factories and stores will have no jobs. Property values in the cities will decline. If, on the other hand, the farms within that area remain as farms with better water supply and no erosion, the farm population will stay on the land and prosper and the nearby cities will prosper too. Property values will increase instead of disappearing. That is why it is worth our while as a nation to spend money in order to save money.

I have used the argument in relation only to a small area. It holds good in its effect on the nation as a whole. Every state in the drought area is now doing and always will do business with every state outside it. The very existence of the men and women working in the clothing factories of New York, making clothes worn by farmers and their families; of the workers in the steel mills in Pittsburgh, in the automobile factories of Detroit, and in the harvester factories of Illinois, depend upon the farmers' ability to purchase the commodities they produce. In the same way it is the purchasing power of the workers in these factories in the cities that enables them and their wives and children to eat more beef, more pork, more wheat, more corn, more fruit and more dairy products, and to buy more clothing made from cotton, wool and leather. In a physical and a property sense, as well as in a spiritual sense, we are members one of another.

I want to make it clear that no simple panacea can be applied to the drought problem in the whole of the drought area. Plans must depend on local conditions, for these vary with annual rainfall, soil characteristics, altitude and topography. Water and soil conservation methods may differ in one county from those in an adjoining county. Work to be done in the cattle and sheep country differs in type from work in the wheat country or work in the corn belt.

The Great Plains Drought Area Committee has given me its preliminary recommendations for a long-time program for that region. Using that report as a basis we are cooperating successfully and in entire accord with the governors and state planning boards. As we get this program into operation the people more and more will be able to maintain themselves securely on the land. That will mean a steady decline in the relief burdens which the federal government and states have had to assume in time of drought; but, more important, it will mean a greater contribution to general national prosperity by these regions which have been hit by drought. It will conserve and improve not only property values, but human values. The people in the drought area do not want to be dependent on federal, state or any other kind of charity. They want for themselves and their families an opportunity to share fairly by their own efforts in the progress of America.

The farmers of America want a sound national agricultural policy in which a permanent land-use program will have an important place. They want assurance against another year like 1932 when they made good crops but had to sell them for prices that meant ruin just as surely as did the drought. Sound policy must maintain farm prices in good crop years as well as in bad crop years. It must function when we have drought; it must also function when we have bumper crops.

The maintenance of a fair equilibrium between farm prices and the prices of industrial products is an aim which we must keep ever before us, just as we must give constant thought to the sufficiency of the food supply of the nation even in bad years. Our modern civilization can and should devise a more successful means by which the excess supplies of bumper years can be conserved for use in lean years.

On my trip I have been deeply impressed with the general efficiency of those agencies of the federal, state and local governments which have moved in on the immediate task created by the drought. In 1934 none of us had preparation; we worked without blueprints and made the mistakes of inexperience. Hindsight shows us this. But as time has gone on we have been making fewer and fewer mistakes. Remember that the federal and state governments have done only broad planning. Actual work on a given project originates in the local community. Local needs are listed from local information. Local projects are decided on only after obtaining the recommendations and help of those in the local community who are best able to give it. And it is worthy of note that on my entire trip, though I asked the question dozens of times, I heard no complaint against the character of a single work relief project.

The elected heads of the states concerned, together with their state officials and their experts from agricultural colleges and state planning boards, have shown cooperation with and approval of the work which the federal government has headed. I am grateful also to the men and women in all these states who have accepted leadership in the work in their locality.

In the drought area people are not afraid to use new methods to meet changes in Nature, and to correct mistakes of the past. If overgrazing has injured range lands, they are willing to reduce the grazing. If certain wheat lands should be returned to pasture they are willing to cooperate. If trees should be planted as windbreaks or to stop erosion they will work with us. If terracing or summer fallowing or crop rotation is called for, they will carry them out. They stand ready to fit, and not to fight, the ways of Nature.

We are helping, and shall continue to help the farmer to do those things, through local soil conservation committees and other cooperative local, state and federal agencies of government.

I have not the time tonight to deal with other and more comprehensive agricultural policies.

With this fine help we are tiding over the present emergency. We are going to conserve soil, conserve water and conserve life. We are going to have long-time defenses against both low prices and drought. We are going to have a farm policy that will serve the national welfare. That is our hope for the future.

There are two reasons why I want to end by talking about reemployment. Tomorrow is Labor Day. The brave spirit with which so many millions of working people are winning their way out of depression deserves respect and admiration. It is like the courage of the farmers in the drought areas.

That is my first reason. The second is that healthy employment conditions stand equally with healthy agricultural conditions as a buttress of national prosperity. Dependable employment at fair wages is just as important to the people in the towns and cities as good farm income is to agriculture. Our people must have the ability to buy the goods they manufacture and the crops they produce. Thus city wages and farm buying power are the two strong legs that carry the nation forward.

Reemployment in industry is proceeding rapidly. Government spending was in large part responsible for keeping industry going and putting it in a position to make this reemployment possible. Government orders were the backlog of heavy industry; government wages turned over and over again to make consumer purchasing power and to sustain every merchant in the community.

Businessmen with their businesses, small and large, had to be saved. Private enterprise is necessary to any nation which seeks to maintain the democratic form of government. In their case, just as certainly as in the case of drought-stricken farmers, government spending has saved.

Government having spent wisely to save it, private industry begins to take workers off the rolls of the government relief program. Until this administration we had no free employment service, except in a few states and cities. Because there was no unified employment service, the worker, forced to move as industry moved, often travelled over the country, wandering after jobs which seemed always to travel just a little faster than he did. He was often victimized by fraudulent practices of employment clearing houses, and the facts of employment opportunities were at the disposal neither of himself nor of the employer.

In 1933 the United States Employment Service was created—a cooperative state and federal enterprise, through which the federal government matches dollar for dollar the funds provided by the states for registering the occupations and skills of workers and for actually finding jobs for these registered workers in private industry. The federal-state cooperation has been splendid. Already employment services are operating in thirty-two states, and the areas not covered by them are served by the federal government.

We have developed a nationwide service with seven hundred district offices and one thousand branch offices, thus providing facilities through which labor can learn of jobs available and employers can find workers.

Last spring I expressed the hope that employers would realize their deep responsibility to take men off the relief rolls and give them jobs in private enterprise. Subsequently I was told by many employers that they were not satisfied with the information available concerning the skill and experience of the workers on the relief rolls. On August 25th I allocated a relatively small sum to the employment service for the purpose of getting better and more recent information in regard to those now actively at work on W.P.A. Projects—information as to their skills and previous occupations—and to keep the records of such men and women up-to-date for maximum service in making them available to industry. Tonight I am announcing the allocation of two and a half million dollars more to enable the Employment Service to make an even more intensive search then it has yet been equipped to make, to find opportunities in private employment for workers registered with it.

Tonight I urge the workers to cooperate with and take full advantage of this intensification of the work of the Employment Service. This does not mean that there will be any lessening of our efforts under our W.P.A. and P.W.A. and other work relief programs until all workers have decent jobs in private employment at decent wages. We do not surrender our responsibility to the unemployed. We have had ample proof that it is the will of the American people that those who represent them in national, state and local government should continue as long as necessary to discharge that responsibility. But it does mean that the government wants to use resource to get private work for those now employed on government work, and thus to curtail to a minimum the government expenditures for direct employment.

Tonight I ask employers, large and small, throughout the nation, to use the help of the state and Federal Employment Service whenever in the general pick-up of business they require more workers.

Tomorrow is Labor Day. Labor Day in this country has never been a class holiday. It has always been a national holiday. It has never had more significance as a national holiday than it has now. In other countries the relationship of employer and employee has been more or less been accepted as a class relationship not readily to be broken through. In this country we insist, as an essential of the American way of life, that the employer-employee relationship should be one between free men and equals. We refuse to regard those who work with hand or brain as different from or inferior to those who live from their property. We insist that labor is entitled to as much respect as property. But our workers with hand and brain deserve more than respect for their labor. They deserve practical protection in the opportunity to use their labor at a return adequate to support them at a decent and constantly rising standard of living, and to accumulate a margin of security against the inevitable vicissitudes of life.

The average man must have that twofold opportunity if we are to avoid the growth of a class-conscious society in this country.

There are those who fail to read both the signs of the times and American history. They would try to refuse the worker any effective power to bargain collectively, to earn a decent livelihood and to acquire security. It is those short-sighted ones, not labor, who threaten this country with that class dissension which in other countries has led to dictatorship and the establishment of fear and hatred as the dominant emotions in human life.

All American workers, brain workers and manual workers alike, and all the rest of us whose well-being depends on theirs, know that our needs are one in building an orderly economic democracy in which all can profit and in which all can be secure from the kind of faulty economic direction which brought us to the brink of common ruin seven years ago.

There is no cleavage between white collar workers and manual workers, between artists and artisans, musicians and mechanics, lawyers and accountants and architects and miners.

Tomorrow, Labor Day, belongs to all of us. Tomorrow, Labor Day, symbolizes the hope of all Americans. Anyone who calls it a class holiday challenges the whole concept of American democracy.

The Fourth of July commemorates our political freedom—a freedom which without economic freedom is meaningless indeed. Labor Day symbolizes our determination to achieve an economic freedom for the average man which will give his political freedom reality.

March 9, 1937.

Last Thursday I described in detail certain economic problems which everyone admits now face the nation. For the many messages which have come to me after that speech, and which it is physically impossible to answer individually, I take this means of saying "thank you."

Tonight, sitting at my desk in the White House, I make my first radio report to the people in my second term of office.

I am reminded of that evening in March, four years ago, when I made my first radio report to you. We were then in the midst of the great banking crisis.

Soon after, with the authority of the Congress, we asked the nation to turn over all of its privately held gold, dollar for dollar, to the government of the United States.

Today's recovery proves how right that policy was.

But when, almost two years later, it came before the Supreme Court its constitutionality was upheld only by a five-to-four vote. The change of one vote would have thrown all the affairs of this great Nation back into hopeless chaos.

In effect, four Justices ruled that the right under a private contract to exact a pound of flesh was more sacred than the main objectives of the Constitution to establish an enduring Nation.

In 1933 you and I knew that we must never let our economic system get completely out of joint again—that we could not afford to take the risk of another great depression.

We also became convinced that the only way to avoid a repetition of those dark days was to have a government with power to prevent and to cure the abuses and the inequalities which had thrown that system out of joint.

We then began a program of remedying those abuses and inequalities—to give balance and stability to our economic system—to make it bomb-proof against the causes of 1929.

Today we are only part-way through that program—and recovery is speeding up to a point where the dangers of 1929 are again becoming possible, not this week or month perhaps, but within a year or two.

National laws are needed to complete that program. Individual or local or state effort alone cannot protect us in 1937 any better than ten years ago.

It will take time—and plenty of time—to work out our remedies administratively even after legislation is passed. To complete our program of protection in time, therefore, we cannot delay one moment in making certain that our national government has power to carry through.

Four years ago action did not come until the eleventh hour. It was almost too late.

If we learned anything from the depression we will not allow ourselves to run around in new circles of futile discussion and debate, always postponing the day of decision.

The American people have learned from the depression. For in the last three national elections an overwhelming majority of them voted a mandate that the Congress and the President begin the task of providing that protection—not after long years of debate, but now.

The courts, however, have cast doubts on the ability of the elected Congress to protect us against catastrophe by meeting squarely our modern social and economic conditions.

We are at a crisis in our ability to proceed with that protection. It is a quiet crisis. There are no lines of depositors outside closed banks. But to the far-sighted it is far-reaching in its possibilities of injury to America.

I want to talk with you very simply about the need for present action in this crisis—the need to meet the unanswered challenge of one-third of a Nation ill-nourished, ill-clad, ill-housed.

Last Thursday I described the American form of government as a three horse team provided by the Constitution to the American people so that their field might be plowed. The three horses are, of course, the three branches of government—the Congress, the Executive and the courts. Two of the horses are pulling in unison today; the third is not. Those who have intimated that the President of the United States is trying to drive that team, overlook the simple fact that the President, as Chief Executive, is himself one of the three horses.

It is the American people themselves who are in the driver's seat.

It is the American people themselves who want the furrow plowed.

It is the American people themselves who expect the third horse to pull in unison with the other two.

I hope that you have re-read the Constitution of the United States in these past few weeks. Like the Bible, it ought to be read again and again.

It is an easy document to understand when you remember that it was called into being because the Articles of Confederation under which the original thirteen States tried to operate after the Revolution showed the need of a national government with power enough to handle national problems. In its Preamble, the Constitution states that it was intended to form a more perfect Union and promote the general welfare; and the powers given to the Congress to carry out those purposes can be best described by saying that they were all the powers needed to meet each and every problem which then had a national character and which could not be met by merely local action.

But the framers went further. Having in mind that in succeeding generations many other problems then undreamed of would become national problems, they gave to the Congress the ample broad powers "to levy taxes . . . and provide for the common defense and general welfare of the United States."

That, my friends, is what I honestly believe to have been the clear and underlying purpose of the patriots who wrote a federal constitution to create a national government with national power, intended as they said, "to form a more perfect union . . . for ourselves and our posterity."

For nearly twenty years there was no conflict between the Congress and the Court. Then Congress passed a statute which, in 1803, the Court said violated an express provision of the Constitution. The Court claimed the power to declare it unconstitutional and did so declare it. But a little later the Court itself admitted that it was an extraordinary power to exercise and through Mr. Justice Washington laid down this limitation upon it: "It is but a decent respect due to the wisdom, the integrity and the patriotism of the legislative body, by which any law is passed, to presume in favor of its validity until its violation of the Constitution is proved beyond all reasonable doubt."

But since the rise of the modern movement for social and economic progress through legislation, the Court has more and more often and more and more boldly asserted a power to veto laws passed by the Congress and state legislatures in complete disregard of this original limitation.

In the last four years the sound rule of giving statutes the benefit of all reasonable doubt has been cast aside. The Court has been acting not as a judicial body, but as a policy-making body.

When the Congress has sought to stabilize national agriculture, to improve the conditions of labor, to safeguard business against unfair competition, to protect our national resources, and in many other ways, to serve our clearly national needs, the majority of the Court has been assuming the power to pass on the wisdom of these acts of the Congress—and to approve or disapprove the public policy written into these laws.

That is not only my accusation. It is the accusation of most distinguished justices of the present Supreme Court. I have not the time to quote to you all the language used by dissenting justices in many of these cases. But in the case holding the Railroad Retirement Act unconstitutional, for instance, Chief Justice Hughes said in a dissenting opinion that the majority opinion was "a departure from sound principles," and placed "an unwarranted limitation upon the commerce clause." And three other justices agreed with him.

In the case of holding the A.A.A. unconstitutional, Justice Stone said of the majority opinion that it was a "tortured construction of the Constitution." And two other justices agreed with him.

In the case holding the New York Minimum Wage Law unconstitutional, Justice Stone said that the majority were actually reading into the Constitution their own "personal economic predilections," and that if the legislative power is not left free to choose the methods of solving the problems of poverty, subsistence, and health of large numbers in the community, then "government is to be rendered impotent." And two other justices agreed with him.

In the face of these dissenting opinions, there is no basis for the claim made by some members of the Court that something in the Constitution has compelled them regretfully to thwart the will of the people.

In the face of such dissenting opinions, it is perfectly clear that, as Chief Justice Hughes has said, "We are under a Constitution, but the Constitution is what the judges say it is."

The Court in addition to the proper use of its judicial functions has improperly set itself up as a third house of the Congress—a super-legislature, as one of the justices has called it—reading into the Constitution words and implications which are not there, and which were never intended to be there.

We have, therefore, reached the point as a nation where we must take action to save the Constitution from the Court and the Court from itself. We must find a way to take an appeal from the Supreme Court to the Constitution itself. We want a Supreme Court which will do justice under the Constitution—not over it. In our courts we want a government of laws and not of men.

I want—as all Americans want—an independent judiciary as proposed by the framers of the Constitution. That means a Supreme Court that will enforce the Constitution as written—that will refuse to amend the Constitution by the arbitrary exercise of judicial power—amended by judicial say-so. It does not mean a judiciary so independent that it can deny the existence of facts which are universally recognized.

How then could we proceed to perform the mandate given us? It was said in last year's Democratic platform, "If these problems cannot be effectively solved within the Constitution, we shall seek such clarifying amendment as will assure the power to enact those laws, adequately to regulate commerce, protect public health and safety, and safeguard economic security." In other words, we said we would seek an amendment only if every other possible means by legislation were to fail.

When I commenced to review the situation with the problem squarely before me, I came by a process of elimination to the conclusion that, short of amendments, the only method which was clearly constitutional, and would at the same time carry out other much needed reforms, was to infuse new blood into all our courts. We must have men worthy and equipped to carry out impartial justice. But, at the same time, we must have judges who will bring to the courts a present-day sense of the Constitution—judges who will retain in the courts the judicial functions of a court, and reject the legislative powers which the courts have today assumed.

In forty-five out of the forty-eight states of the Union, judges are chosen not for life but for a period of years. In many states judges must retire at the age of seventy. Congress has provided financial security by offering life pensions at full pay for federal judges on all courts who are willing to retire at seventy. In the case of Supreme Court justices, that pension is $20,000 a year. But all federal judges, once appointed, can, if they choose, hold office for life, no matter how old they may get to be.

What is my proposal? It is simply this: whenever a judge or justice of any federal court has reached the age of seventy and does not avail himself of the opportunity to retire on a pension, a new member shall be appointed by the President then in office, with the approval, as required by the Constitution, of the Senate of the United States.

That plan has two chief purposes. By bringing into the judicial system a steady and continuing stream of new and younger blood, I hope, first, to make the administration of all federal justice speedier and, therefore, less costly; secondly, to bring to the decision of social and economic problems younger men who have had personal experience and contact with modern facts and circumstances under which average men have to live and work. This plan will save our national Constitution from hardening of the judicial arteries.

The number of judges to be appointed would depend wholly on the decision of present judges now over seventy, or those who would subsequently reach the age of seventy.

If, for instance, any one of the six justices of the Supreme Court now over the age of seventy should retire as provided under the plan, no additional place would be created. Consequently, although there never can be more than fifteen, there may be only fourteen, or thirteen, or twelve. And there may be only nine.

There is nothing novel or radical about this idea. It seeks to maintain the federal bench in full vigor. It has been discussed and approved by many persons of high authority ever since a similar proposal passed the House of Representatives in 1869.

Why was the age fixed at seventy? Because the laws of many states, the practice of the Civil Service, the regulations of the Army and Navy, and the rules of many of our universities and of almost every great private business enterprise, commonly fix the retirement age at seventy years or less.

The statute would apply to all the courts in the federal system. There is general approval so far as the lower federal courts are concerned. The plan has met opposition only so far as the Supreme Court of the United States itself is concerned. If such a plan is good for the lower courts it certainly ought to be equally good for the highest court from which there is no appeal.

Those opposing this plan have sought to arouse prejudice and fear by crying that I am seeking to "pack" the Supreme Court and that a baneful precedent will be established.

What do they mean by the words "packing the Court"?

Let me answer this question with a bluntness that will end all *honest* misunderstanding of my purposes.

If by that phrase "packing the Court" it is charged that I wish to place on the bench spineless puppets who would disregard the law and would decide specific cases as I wished them to be decided, I make this answer: that no President fit for his office would appoint, and no Senate of honorable men fit for their office would confirm, that kind of appointees to the Supreme Court.

But if by that phrase the charge is made that I would appoint and the Senate would confirm justices worthy to sit beside present members of the Court who understand those modern conditions, that I will appoint justices who will not undertake to override the judgment of the Congress on legislative policy, that I will appoint justices who will act as justices and not as legislators—if the appointment of such justices can be called "packing the Courts," then I say that I and with me the vast majority of the American people favor doing just that thing—now.

Is it a dangerous precedent for the Congress to change the number of the justices? The Congress has always had, and will have, that power. The number of justices has been changed several times before, in the administration of John Adams and Thomas Jefferson—both signers of the Declaration of Independence—Andrew Jackson, Abraham Lincoln and Ulysses S. Grant.

I suggest only the addition of justices to the bench in accordance with a clearly defined principle relating to a clearly defined age limit. Fundamentally, if in the future, America cannot trust the Congress it elects to refrain from abuse of our Constitutional usages, democracy will have failed far beyond the importance to it of any king of precedent concerning the judiciary.

We think it so much in the public interest to maintain a vigorous judiciary that we encourage the retirement of elderly judges by offering them a life pension at full salary. Why then should we leave the fulfillment of this public policy to chance or make independent on upon the desire or prejudice of any individual justice?

It is the clear intention of our public policy to provide for a constant flow of new and younger blood into the judiciary. Normally every President appoints a large number of district and circuit court judges and a few members of the Supreme Court. Until my first term practically every President of the United States has appointed at least one member of the Supreme Court. President Taft appointed five members and named a Chief Justice; President Wilson, three; President Harding, four, including a Chief Justice; President Coolidge, one; President Hoover, three, including a Chief Justice.

Such a succession of appointments should have provided a Court well-balanced as to age. But chance and the disinclination of individuals to leave the Supreme bench have now given us a Court in which five justices will be over seventy-five years of age before next June and one over seventy. Thus a sound public policy has been defeated.

I now propose that we establish by law an assurance against any such ill-balanced court in the future. I propose that hereafter, when a judge reaches the age of seventy, a new and younger judge shall be added to the court automatically. In this way I propose to enforce a sound public policy by law instead of leaving the composition of our federal courts, including the highest, to be determined by chance or the personal indecision of individuals.

If such a law as I propose is regarded as establishing a new precedent, is it not a most desirable precedent?

Like all lawyers, like all Americans, I regret the necessity of this controversy. But the welfare of the United States, and indeed of the Constitution itself, is what we all must think about first. Our difficulty with the Court today rises not from the Court as an institution but from human beings within it. But we cannot yield our constitutional destiny to the personal judgment of a few men who, being fearful of the future, would deny us the necessary means of dealing with the present.

This plan of mine is no attack on the Court; it seeks to restore the Court to its rightful and historic place in our constitutional government and to have it resume its high task of building anew on the Constitution "a system of living law." The Court itself can best undo what the Court has done.

I have thus explained to you the reasons that lie behind our efforts to secure results by legislation within the Constitution. I hope that thereby the difficult process of constitutional amendment may be rendered unnecessary. But let us examine the process.

There are many types of amendment proposed. Each one is radically different from the other. There is no substantial groups within the Congress or outside it who are agreed on any single amendment.

It would take months or years to get substantial agreement upon the type and language of the amendment. It would take months and years thereafter to get a two-thirds majority in favor of that amendment in *both* Houses of the Congress.

Then would come the long course of ratification by three-fourths of all the states. No amendment which any powerful economic interests or the leaders of any powerful political party have had reason to oppose has ever been ratified within anything like a reasonable time. And thirteen states which contain only five percent of the voting population can block ratification even though the thirty- five states with ninety-five percent of the population are in favor of it.

A very large percentage of newspaper publishers, Chambers of Commerce, Bar Association, Manufacturers' Associations, who are trying to give the impression that they really do want a constitutional amendment would be the first to exclaim as soon as an amendment was proposed, "Oh! I was for an amendment all right, but this amendment you proposed is not the kind of amendment that I was thinking about. I am therefore, going to spend my time, my efforts and my money to block the amendment, although I would be awfully glad to help get some other kind of amendment ratified."

Two groups oppose my plan on the ground that they favor a constitutional amendment. The first includes those who fundamentally object to social and economic legislation along modern lines. This is the same group who during the campaign last Fall tried to block the mandate of the people.

Now they are making a last stand. And the strategy of that last stand is to suggest the time-consuming process of amendment in order to kill off by delay the legislation demanded by the mandate.

To them I say: I do not think you will be able long to fool the American people as to your purposes.

The other groups is composed of those who honestly believe the amendment process is the best and who would be willing to support a reasonable amendment if they could agree on one.

To them I say: we cannot rely on an amendment as the immediate or only answer to our present difficulties. When the time comes for action, you will find that many of those who pretend to support you will sabotage any constructive amendment which is proposed. Look at these strange bed-fellows of yours. When before have you found them really at your side in your fights for progress?

And remember one thing more. Even if an amendment were passed, and even if in the years to come it were to be ratified, its meaning would depend upon the kind of justices who would be sitting on the Supreme Court bench. An amendment, like the rest of the Constitution, is what the justices say it is rather than what its framers or you might hope it is.

This proposal of mine will not infringe in the slightest upon the civil or religious liberties so dear to every American.

My record as Governor and President proves my devotion to those liberties. You who know me can have no fear that I would tolerate the destruction by any branch of government of any part of our heritage of freedom.

The present attempt by those opposed to progress to play upon the fears of danger to personal liberty brings again to mind that crude and cruel strategy tried by the same opposition to frighten the workers of America in a pay-envelope propaganda against the Social Security Law. The workers were not fooled by that propaganda then. The people of America will not be fooled by such propaganda now.

I am in favor of action through legislation:

First, because I believe that it can be passed at this session of the Congress.
Second, because it will provide a reinvigorated, liberal-minded judiciary necessary to furnish quicker and cheaper justice from bottom to top.
Third, because it will provide a series of federal courts willing to enforce the Constitution as written, and unwilling to assert legislative powers by writing into it their own political and economic policies.

During the past half century the balance of power between the three great branches of the federal government, has been tipped out of balance by the courts in direct contradiction of the high purposes of the framers of the Constitution. It is my purpose to restore that balance. You who know me will accept my solemn assurance that in a world in which democracy is under attack, I seek to make American democracy succeed. You and I will do our part.

October 12, 1937.

My Friends:

This afternoon I have issued a Proclamation calling a special session of the Congress to convene on Monday, November 15, 1937.

I do this in order to give to the Congress an opportunity to consider important legislation before the regular session in January, and to enable the Congress to avoid a lengthy session next year, extending through the summer.

I know that many enemies of democracy will say that it is bad for business, bad for the tranquility of the country, to have a special session—even one beginning only six weeks before the regular session. But I have never had sympathy with the point of view that a session of the Congress is an unfortunate intrusion of what they call "politics" into our national affairs. Those who do not like democracy want to keep legislators at home. But the Congress is an essential instrument of democratic government; and democratic government can never be considered an intruder into the affairs of a democratic nation.

I shall ask this special session to consider immediately certain important legislation which my recent trip through the nation convinces me the American people immediately need. This does not mean that other legislation, to which I am not referring tonight, is not important for our national well-being. But other legislation can be more readily discussed at the regular session.

Anyone charged with proposing or judging national policies should have first-hand knowledge of the nation as a whole.

That is why again this year I have taken trips to all parts of the country. Last spring I visited the Southwest. This summer I made several trips in the East. Now I am just back from a trip from a trip all the way across the continent, and later this autumn I hope to pay my annual visit to the Southeast.

For a President especially it is a duty to think in national terms.

He must think not only of this year but of future years, when someone else will be President.

He must look beyond the average of the prosperity and well-being of the country, for averages easily cover up danger spots of poverty and instability.

He must not let the country be deceived by a merely temporary prosperity which depends on wasteful exploitation of resources which cannot last.

He must think not only of keeping us out of war today, but also of keeping us out of war in generations to come.

The kind of prosperity we want is the sound and permanent kind which is not built up temporarily at the expense of any section or any group. And the kind of peace we want is the sound and permanent kind, which is built on the cooperative search for peace by all the nations which want peace.

The other day I was asked to state my outstanding impression gained on this recent trip. I said that it seemed to me to be the general understanding on the part of the average citizen of the broad objectives and policies which I have just outlined.

Five years of fierce discussion and debate—five years of information through the radio and the moving picture—have taken the whole nation to school in the nation's business. Even those who have most attacked our objectives have, by their very criticism, encouraged the mass of our citizens to think about and understand the issues involved, and, understanding, to approve.

Out of that process, we have learned to think as a nation. And out of that process we have learned to feel ourselves a nation. As never before in our history, each section of America says to every other section, "Thy people shall be my people."

For most of the country this has been a good year—better in dollars and cents than for many years—far better in the soundness of its prosperity. And everywhere I went I found particular optimism about the good effect on business which is expected from the steady spending by farmers of the largest farm income in many years.

But we have not yet done all that must be done to make this prosperity stable. The people of the United States were checked in their efforts to prevent future piling up of huge agricultural surpluses and the tumbling prices which inevitably follow them. They were checked in their efforts to secure reasonable minimum wages and maximum hours and the end of child labor. And because they were checked, many groups in many parts of the country still have less purchasing power and a lower standard of living than the nation as a whole can permanently allow.

Americans realize these facts. That is why they ask government not to stop governing simply because prosperity has come back a long way.

They do not look on government as an interloper in their affairs. On the contrary, they regard it as the most effective form of organized self-help.

Sometimes I get bored sitting in Washington hearing certain people talk and talk about all that government ought *not* do—people who got all *they* wanted from government back in the days when the financial institutions and the railroads were being bailed out by the government in 1933. It is refreshing to go out through the country and feel the common wisdom that the time to repair the roof is when the sun is shining.

They want the financial budget balanced. But they want the human budget balanced as well. They want to set up a national economy which balances itself with as little government subsidy as possible, for they realize that persistent subsidies ultimately bankrupt their government.

They are less concerned that every detail be immediately right than they are that the direction be right. They know that just so long as we are traveling on the right road, it does not make much difference if occasionally we hit a "Thank you marm."

The overwhelming majority of our citizens who live by agriculture are thinking very clearly how they want government to help them in connection with the production of crops. They want government help in two ways: first, in the control of surpluses, and, second, in the proper use of land.

The other day a reporter told me that he had never been able to understand why the government seeks to curtail crop production and, at the same time, to open up new irrigated acres.

He was confusing two totally separate objectives.

Crop surplus control relates to the total amount of any major crop grown in the whole nation on all cultivated land—good or bad—control by the cooperation of the crop growers and with the help of the government. Land use, on the other hand, is a policy of providing each farmer with the best quality and type of land we have, or can make available, for his part in that total production. Adding good new land for diversified crops is offset by abandoning poor land now uneconomically farmed.

The total amount of production largely determines the price of the crop, and, therefore, the difference between comfort and misery for the farmer.

If we Americans were foolish enough to run every shoe factory twenty-four hours a day, seven days a week, we would soon have more shoes than the nation could possibly buy—a surplus of shoes so great that it would have to be destroyed, or given away, or sold at prices far below the cost of production. That simple law of supply and demand equally affects the price of all our major crops.

You and I have heard big manufacturers talk about control of production by the farmer as an indefensible "economy of scarcity." And yet these same manufacturers never hesitate to shut down their own huge plants, throw men out of work, and cut down the purchasing power of whole communities whenever they think that they must adjust their production to an oversupply of the goods they make. When it is their baby who has the measles, they call it not "an economy of scarcity" but "sound business judgment."

Of course, speaking seriously, what you and I want is such governmental rules of the game that labor and agriculture and industry will all produce a balanced abundance without waste.

So we intend this winter to find a way to prevent four-and-a-half cent cotton, nine cent corn and thirty cent wheat—with all the disaster those prices mean for all of us—to prevent those prices from ever coming back again. To do that, the farmers themselves want to cooperate to build an all-weather farm program so that in the long run prices will be more stable. They believe this can be done, and the national budget kept out of the red.

And when we have found that way to protect the farmers' prices from the effects of alternating crop surpluses and crop scarcities, we shall also have found the way to protect the nation's food supply from the effects of the same fluctuation. We ought always to have enough food at prices within the reach of the consuming public. For the consumers in the cities of America, we must find a way to help the farmers to store up in years of plenty enough to avoid hardship in the years of scarcity.

Our land use policy is a different thing. I have just visited much of the work that the national government is doing to stop soil erosion, to save our forests, to prevent floods, to produce electric power for more general use, and to give people a chance to move from poor land on to better land by irrigating thousands of acres that need only water to provide an opportunity to make a good living.

I saw bare and burned hillsides where only a few years ago great forests were growing. They are now being planted to young trees, not only to stop erosion, but to provide a lumber supply for the future.

I saw C.C.C. boys and W.P.A. workers building check-dams and small ponds and terraces to raise the water table and make it possible for farms and villages to remain in safety where they now are. I saw the harnessing of the turbulent Missouri, muddy with the topsoil of many states. And I saw barges on new channels carrying produce and freight athwart the nation.

Let me give you two simple illustrations of why government projects of this type have a national importance for the whole country.

In the Boise Valley in Idaho I saw a district which had been recently irrigated to enormous fertility so that a family can now make a pretty good living from forty acres of its land. Many of the families, who are making good in that valley today, moved there from a thousand miles away. They came from the dust strip that runs through the middle of the nation all the way from the Canadian border to Mexico, a strip which includes large portions of ten states. That valley in western Idaho, therefore, assumes at once a national importance as a second chance for willing farmers. And, year by year, we propose to add more valleys to take care of thousands of other families who need the same kind of second chance in new green pastures.

The other illustration was at the Grand Coulee Dam in the state of Washington. The engineer in charge told me that almost half of the whole cost of that dam to date had been spent for materials that were manufactured east of the Mississippi River, giving employment and wages to thousands of industrial workers in the eastern third of the nation, two thousand miles away.

All of this work needs, of course, a more businesslike system of planning and greater foresight than we use today.

That is why I recommended to the last session of the Congress the creation of seven planning regions, in which local people will originate and coordinate recommendations as to the kind of this work of this kind to be done in their particular regions. The Congress will, of course, determine the projects to be selected within the budget limits.

To carry out any twentieth century program, we must give the Executive branch of the government twentieth century machinery to work with. I recognize that democratic processes are necessarily and rightly slower than dictatorial processes. But I refuse to believe that democratic processes need be dangerously slow.

For many years we have all known that the Executive and Administrative departments of the government in Washington are a higgledy-piggledy patchwork of duplicate responsibilities and overlapping powers. The reorganization of this vast government machinery which I proposed to the Congress last winter does not conflict with the principle of the democratic process, as some people say. It only makes that process work more efficiently.

On my recent trip many people have talked to me about the millions of men and women and children who still work at insufficient wages and overlong hours.

American industry has searched the outside world to find new markets—but it can create on its very doorstep the biggest and most permanent market it has ever had. It needs the reduction of trade barriers to improve its foreign markets, but it should not overlook the chance to reduce the domestic trade barrier right here—right away—without waiting for any treaty. A few more dollars a week in wages, a better distribution of jobs with a shorter working day will almost overnight make millions of our lowest-paid workers actual buyers of billions of dollars of industrial and farm products. That increased volume of sales ought to lessen other cost of production so much that even a considerable increase in labor costs can be absorbed without imposing higher prices on the consumer.

I am a firm believer in fully adequate pay for all labor. But right now I am most greatly concerned in increasing the pay of the lowest-paid labor—those who are our most numerous consuming group but who today do not make enough to maintain a decent standard of living or to buy the food, and the clothes and the other articles necessary to keep our factories and farms fully running.

Farsighted businessmen already understand and agree with this policy. They agree also that no one section of the country can permanently benefit itself, or the rest of the country, by maintaining standards of wages and hours far inferior to other sections of the country.

Most businessmen, big and little, know that their government neither wants to put them out of business nor to prevent them from earning a decent profit. In spite of the alarms of a few who seek to regain control of American life, most businessmen, big and little, know that their government is trying to make property more secure than ever before by giving every family a real chance to have a property stake in the nation.

Whatever danger there may be to the property and profits of the many, if there be any danger, comes not from government's attitude toward business but from restraints now imposed upon business by private monopolies and financial oligarchies. The average businessman knows that a high cost of living is a great deterrent to business and that business prosperity depends much upon a low price policy which encourages the widest possible consumption. As one of the country's leading economists recently said, "The continuance of business recovery in the United States depends far more upon business policies, business pricing policies, than it does on anything that may be done, or not done, in Washington."

Our competitive system is, of course, not altogether competitive. Anybody who buys any large quantity of manufactured goods knows this, whether it be the government or an individual buyer. We have anti-trust laws, to be sure, but they have not been adequate to check the growth of many monopolies. Whether or not they might have been adequate originally, interpretation by the courts and the difficulties and delays of legal procedure have now definitely limited their effectiveness.

We are already studying how to strengthen our anti-trust laws in order to end monopoly—not to hurt but to free legitimate business.

I have touched briefly on these important subjects, which, taken together, make a program for the immediate future. To attain it, legislation is necessary.

As we plan today for the creation of ever higher standards of living for the people of the United States, we are aware that our plans may be most seriously affected by events in the world outside our borders.

By a series of trade agreements, we have been attempting to recreate the trade of the world which plays so important a part in our domestic prosperity; but we know that if the world outside our borders falls into the chaos of war, world trade will be completely disrupted.

Nor can we view with indifference the destruction of civilized values throughout the world. We seek peace, not only for our generation but also for the generation of our children.

We seek for them the continuance of world civilization in order that their American civilization may continue to be invigorated by the achievements of civilized men and women in the rest of the world.

I want our great democracy to be wise enough to realize that aloofness from war is not promoted by unawareness of war. In a world of mutual suspicions, peace must be affirmatively reached for. It cannot just be wished for. And it cannot just be waited for.

We have now made known our willingness to attend a conference of the parties to the Nine Power Treaty of 1922—the Treaty of Washington—of which we are one of the original signatories. The purpose of this conference will be to seek by agreement a solution of the present situation in China. In efforts to find that solution, it is our purpose to cooperate with the other signatories to this Treaty, including China and Japan.

Such cooperation would be an example of one of the possible paths to follow in our search for means toward peace throughout the whole world.

The development of civilization and of human welfare is based on the acceptance by individuals of certain fundamental decencies in their relations with each other. The development of peace in the world is dependent similarly on the acceptance by nations of certain fundamental decencies in their relations with each other.

Ultimately, I hope *each* nation will accept the fact that violations of these rules of conduct are an injury to the well- being of *all* nations.

Meanwhile, remember that from 1913 to 1921, I personally was fairly close to world events, and in that period, while I learned much of what to do, I also learned much of what *not* to do.

The common sense, the intelligence of America agree with my statement that "America hates war. America hopes for peace. Therefore, America actively engages in the search for peace."

April 14, 1938.

My Friends:

Five months have gone by since I last spoke to the people of the nation about the state of the nation.

I had hoped to be able to defer this talk until next week because, as we all know, this is Holy Week. But what I want to say to you, the people of the country, is of such immediate need and relates so closely to the lives of human beings and the prevention of human suffering that I have felt that there should be no delay. In this decision I have been strengthened by the thought that by speaking tonight there may be greater peace of mind and that the hope of Easter may be more real at firesides everywhere, and therefore that it is not inappropriate to encourage peace when so many of us are thinking of the Prince of Peace.

Five years ago we faced a very serious problem of economic and social recovery. For four and a half years that recovery proceeded apace. It is only in the past seven months that it has received a visible setback.

And it is only within the past two months, as we have waited patiently to see whether the forces of business itself would counteract it, that it has become apparent that government itself can no longer safely fail to take aggressive government steps to meet it.

This recession has not returned us the disasters and suffering of the beginning of 1933. Your money in the bank is safe; farmers are no longer in deep distress and have greater purchasing power; dangers of security speculation have been minimized; national income is almost 50 percent higher than in 1932; and government has an established and accepted responsibility for relief.

But I know that many of you have lost your jobs or have seen your friends or members of your families lose their jobs, and I do not propose that the government shall pretend not to see these things. I know that the effect of our present difficulties has been uneven; that they have affected some groups and some localities seriously, but that they have been scarcely felt in others. But I conceive the first duty of government is to protect the economic welfare of all the people in all sections and in all groups. I said in my message opening the last session of the Congress that if private enterprise did not provide jobs this spring, government would take up the slack—that I would not let the people down. We have all learned the lesson that government cannot afford to wait until it has lost the power to act.

Therefore, my friends, I have sent a message of far-reaching importance to the Congress. I want to read to you tonight certain passages from that message, and to talk with you about them.

In that message I analyzed the causes of the collapse of 1929 in these words: "over-speculation in and overproduction of practically every article or instrument used by man . . . millions of people, to be sure, had been put to work, but the products of their hands had exceeded the purchasing power of their pocketbooks . . . Under the inexorable law of supply and demand, supplies so overran demand which would pay that production was compelled to stop. Unemployment and closed factories resulted. Hence the tragic years from 1929 to 1933."

I pointed out to the Congress that the national income—not the government's income but the total of the income of all the individual citizens and families of the United States—every farmer, every worker, every banker, every professional man and every person who lived on income derived from investments—that national income had amounted, in the year 1929, to eighty-one billion dollars. By 1932 this had fallen to thirty-eight billion dollars. Gradually, and up to a few months ago, it had risen to a total, an annual total; of sixty-eight billion dollars—a pretty good come-back from the low point.

I then said this to the Congress:

"But the very vigor of the recovery in both durable goods and consumers' goods brought into the picture early in certain highly undesirable practices, which were in large part responsible for the economic decline which began in the later months of that year. Again production outran the ability to buy.

"There were many reasons for this overproduction. One of them was fear—fear of war abroad, fear of inflation, fear of nation-wide strikes. None of these fears have been borne out.

" . . . Production in many important lines of goods outran the ability of the public to purchase them. For example, through the winter and spring of 1937 cotton factories in hundreds of cases were running on a three-shift basis, piling up cotton goods in the factory, and in the hands of middle men and retailers. For example, also, automobile manufacturers not only turned out a normal increase of finished cars, but encouraged the normal increase to run into abnormal figures, using every known method to push their sales. This meant, of course, that the steel mills of the nation ran on a twenty-four hour basis, and the tire companies and cotton factories and glass factories and others speeded up to meet the same type of abnormally stimulated demand. The buying power of the nation lagged behind.

"Thus by the autumn of 1937, last autumn, the nation again had stocks on hand which the consuming public could not buy because the purchasing power of the consuming public had not kept pace with the production.

"During the same period . . . the prices of many vital products had risen faster than was warranted . . . In the case of many commodities the price to the consumer was raised well above the inflationary boom prices of 1929. In many lines of goods and materials, prices got so high that buyers and builders ceased to buy or to build.

" . . . The economic process of getting out the raw materials, putting them through the manufacturing and finishing processes, selling them to the retailers, selling them to the consumer, and finally using them, got completely out of balance.

" . . . The laying off of workers came upon us last autumn and has been continuing at such a pace ever since that all of us, government and banking and business and workers, and those faced with destitution, recognize the need for action."

All of this I said to the Congress today and I repeat it to you, the people of the country tonight.

I went on to point out to the Senate and the House of Representatives that all the energies of government and business must be directed to increasing the national income, to putting more people into private jobs, to giving security and a feeling of security to all people in all walks of life.

I am constantly thinking of all our people—unemployed and employed alike—of their human problems of food and clothing and homes and education and health and old age. You and I agree that security is our greatest need; the chance to work, the opportunity of making a reasonable profit in our business—whether it be a very small business or a larger one—the possibility of selling our farm products for enough money for our families to live on decently. I know these are the things that decide the well-being of all our people.

Therefore, I am determined to do all in my power to help you attain that security and because I know that the people themselves have a deep conviction that secure prosperity of that kind cannot be a lasting one except on a basis of business fair dealing and a basis where all from the top to the bottom share in the prosperity. I repeated to the Congress today that neither it nor the Chief Executive can afford "to weaken or destroy great reforms which, during the past five years, have been effected on behalf of the American people. In our rehabilitation of the banking structure and of agriculture, in our provisions for adequate and cheaper credit for all types of business, in our acceptance of national responsibility for unemployment relief, in our strengthening of the credit of state and local government, in our encouragement of housing, and slum clearance and home ownership, in our supervision of stock exchanges and public utility holding companies and the issuance of new securities, in our provision for social security, the electorate of America wants no backward steps taken.

"We have recognized the right of labor to free organization, to collective bargaining; and machinery for the handling of labor relations is now in existence. The principles are established even though we can all admit that, through the evolution of time, administration and practices can be improved. Such improvement can come about most quickly and most peacefully through sincere efforts to understand and assist on the part of labor leaders and employers alike.

"The never-ceasing evolution of human society will doubtless bring forth new problems which will require new adjustments. Our immediate task is to consolidate and maintain the gains achieved.

"In this situation there is no reason and no occasion for any American to allow his fears to be aroused or his energy and enterprise to be paralyzed by doubt or uncertainty."

I came to the conclusion that the present-day problem calls for action both by the government and by the people, that we suffer primarily from a failure of consumer demand because of lack of buying power. Therefore it is up to us to create an economic upturn.

"How and where can and should the government help to start an upward spiral?"

I went on in my message today to propose three groups of measures and I will summarize my recommendations.

First, I asked for certain appropriations which are intended to keep the government expenditures for work relief and similar purposes during the coming fiscal year at the same rate of expenditure as at present. That includes additional money for the Works Progress Administration; additional funds for the Farm Security Administration; additional allotments for the national Youth Administration, and more money for the Civilian Conservation Corps, in order that it can maintain the existing number of camps now in operation.

These appropriations, made necessary by increased unemployment, will cost about a billion and a quarter dollars more than the estimates which I sent to the Congress on the third of January.

Second, I told the Congress that the administration proposes to make additional bank reserves available for the credit needs of the country. About one billion four hundred million dollars of gold now in the treasury will be used to pay these additional expenses of the government, and three-quarters of a billion dollars of additional credit will be made available to the banks by reducing the reserves now required by the Federal Reserve Board.

These two steps—taking care of relief needs and adding to bank credits—are in our best judgment insufficient by themselves to start the nation on a sustained upward movement.

Therefore, I came to the third kind of government action which I consider to be vital. I said to the Congress:

"You and I cannot afford to equip ourselves with two rounds of ammunition where three rounds are necessary. If we stop at relief and credit, we may find ourselves without ammunition before the enemy is routed. If we are fully equipped with the third round of ammunition, we stand to win the battle against adversity."

This third proposal is to make definite additions to the purchasing power of the nation by providing new work over and above the continuing of the old work.

First, to enable the United States Housing Authority to undertake the immediate construction of about three hundred million dollars of additional slum clearance projects.

Second, to renew a public works program by starting as quickly as possible about one billion dollars worth of needed permanent public improvements in our states, and their counties and cities.

Third, to add one hundred million dollars to the estimate for federal aid highways in excess of the amount I recommended in January.

Fourth, to add thirty-seven million dollars over and above the former estimate of sixty-three million for flood control and reclamation.

Fifth, to add twenty-five million dollars additional for federal buildings in various parts of the country.

In recommending this program I am thinking not only of the immediate economic needs of the people of the nation, but also of their personal liberties—the most precious possession of all Americans. I am thinking of our democracy and of the recent trend in other parts of the world away from the democratic ideal.

Democracy has disappeared in several other great nations—disappeared not because the people of those nations disliked democracy, but because they had grown tired of unemployment and insecurity, of seeing their children hungry while they sat helpless in the face of government confusion and government weakness through lack of leadership in government. Finally, in desperation, they chose to sacrifice liberty in the hope of getting something to eat. We in America know that our own democratic institutions can be preserved and made to work. But in order to preserve them we need to act together, to meet the problems of the nation boldly, and to prove that the practical operation of democratic government is equal to the task of protecting the security of the people.

Not only our future economic soundness but the very soundness of our democratic institutions depends on the determination of our government to give employment to idle men. The people of America are in agreement in defending their liberties at any cost, and the first line of that defense lies in the protection of economic security. Your government, seeking to protect democracy, must prove that government is stronger than the forces of business depression.

History proves that dictatorships do not grow out of strong and successful governments but out of weak and helpless governments. If by democratic methods people get a government strong enough to protect them from fear and starvation, their democracy succeeds, but if they do not, they grow impatient. Therefore, the only sure bulwark of continuing liberty is a government strong enough to protect the interests of the people, and a people strong enough and well enough informed to maintain its sovereign control over its government.

We are a rich Nation; we can afford to pay for security and prosperity without having to sacrifice our liberties into the bargain.

In the first century of our republic we were short of capital, short of workers and short of industrial production; but we were rich in free land, free timber and free mineral wealth. The federal government rightly assumed the duty of promoting business and relieving depression by giving subsidies of land and other resources.

Thus, from our earliest days we have had a tradition of substantial government help to our system of private enterprise. But today the government no longer has vast tracts of rich land to give away and we have discovered, too, that we must spend large sums of money to conserve our land from further erosion and our forests from further depletion. The situation is also very different from the old days, because now we have plenty of capital, banks and insurance companies loaded with idle money; plenty of industrial productive capacity and many millions of workers looking for jobs. It is following tradition as well as necessity, if government strives to put idle money and idle men to work, to increase our public wealth and to build up the health and strength of the people—and to help our system of private enterprise to function.

It is going to cost something to get out of this recession this way but the profit of getting out of it will pay for the cost several times over. Lost working time is lost money. Every day that a workman is unemployed, or a machine is unused, or a business organization is marking time, it is a loss to the nation. Because of idle men and idle machines this Nation lost one hundred billion dollars between 1929 and the Spring of 1933, in less than four years. This year you, the people of this country, are making about twelve billion dollars less than last year.

If you think back to the experiences of the early years of this administration you will remember the doubts and fears expressed about the rising expenses of government. But to the surprise of the doubters, as we proceeded to carry on the program which included Public Works and Work Relief, the country grew richer instead of poorer.

It is worthwhile to remember that the annual national people's income was thirty billion dollars more last year in 1937 than it was in 1932. It is true that the national debt increased sixteen billion dollars, but remember that in that increase must be included several billion dollars worth of assets which eventually will reduce that debt and that many billion dollars of permanent public improvements—schools, roads, bridges, tunnels, public buildings, parks and a host of other things—meet your eye in every one of the thirty-one hundred counties in the United States.

No doubt you will be told that the government spending program of the past five years did not cause the increase in our national income. They will tell you that business revived because of private spending and investment. That is true in part, for the government spent only a small part of the total. But that government spending acted as a trigger to set off private activity. That is why the total addition to our national production and national income has been so much greater than the contribution of the government itself.

In pursuance of that thought I said to the Congress today:

"I want to make it clear that we do not believe that we can get an adequate rise in national income merely by investing, and lending or spending public funds. It is essential in our economy that private funds must be put to work and all of us recognize that such funds are entitled to a fair profit."

As national income rises, "let us not forget that government expenditures will go down and government tax receipts will go up."

The government contribution of land that we once made to business was the land of all the people. And the government contribution of money which we now make to business ultimately comes out of the labor of all the people. It is, therefore, only sound morality, as well as a sound distribution of buying power, that the benefits of the prosperity coming from this use of the money of all the people ought to be distributed among all the people—at the bottom as well as at the top. Consequently, I am again expressing my hope that the Congress will enact at this session a wage and hour bill putting a floor under industrial wages and a limit on working hours—to ensure a better distribution of our prosperity, a better distribution of available work, and a sounder distribution of buying power.

You may get all kinds of impressions in regard to the total cost of this new program, or in regard to the amount that will be added to the net national debt.

It is a big program. Last autumn in a sincere effort to bring government expenditures and government income into closer balance, the Budget I worked out called for sharp decreases in government spending.

In the light of present conditions those estimates were far too low. This new program adds two billion and sixty-two million dollars to direct treasury expenditures and another nine hundred and fifty million dollars to government loans—the latter sum, because they are loans, will come back to the treasury in the future.

The net effect on the debt of the government is this—between now and July 1, 1939—fifteen months away—the treasury will have to raise less than a billion and a half dollars of new money.

Such an addition to the net debt of the United States need not give concern to any citizen, for it will return to the people of the United States many times over in increased buying power and eventually in much greater government tax receipts because of the increase in the citizen income.

What I said to the Congress in the close of my message I repeat to you.

"Let us unanimously recognize the fact that the federal debt, whether it be twenty-five billions or forty billions, can only be paid if the nation obtains a vastly increased citizen income. I repeat that if this citizen income can be raised to eighty billion dollars a year the national government and the overwhelming majority of state and local governments will be definitely 'out of the red.' The higher the national income goes the faster will we be able to reduce the total of federal and state and local debts. Viewed from every angle, today's purchasing power—the citizens' income of today—is not at this time sufficient to drive the economic system of America at higher speed. Responsibility of government requires us at this time to supplement the normal processes and in so supplementing them to make sure that the addition is adequate. We must start again on a long steady upward incline in national income.

" . . . And in that process, which I believe is ready to start, let us avoid the pitfalls of the past—the overproduction, the overspeculation, and indeed all the extremes which we did not succeed in avoiding in 1929. In all of this, government cannot and should not act alone. Business must help. And I am sure business will help.

"We need more than the materials of recovery. We need a united national will.

"We need to recognize nationally that the demands of no group, however just, can be satisfied unless that group is prepared to share in finding a way to produce the income from which they and all other groups can be paid . . . You, as the Congress, I, as the President, must by virtue of our offices, seek the national good by preserving the balance between all groups and all sections.

"We have at our disposal the national resources, the money, the skill of hand and head to raise our economic level—our citizens' income. Our capacity is limited only by our ability to work together. What is needed is the will.

"The time has come to bring that will into action with every driving force at our command. And I am determined to do my share.

" . . . Certain positive requirements seem to me to accompany the will—if we have that will.

"There is placed on all of us the duty of self-restraint . . . That is the discipline of a democracy. Every patriotic citizen must say to himself or herself, that immoderate statement, appeals to prejudice, the creation of unkindness, are offenses not against an individual or individuals, but offenses against the whole population of the United States . . .

"Self-restraint implies restraint by articulate public opinion, trained to distinguish fact from falsehood, trained to believe that bitterness is never a useful instrument in public affairs. There can be no dictatorship by an individual or by a group in this Nation, save through division fostered by hate. Such division there must never be."

And finally I should like to say a personal word to you.

I never forget that I live in a house owned by all the American people and that I have been given their trust.

I try always to remember that their deepest problems are human. I constantly talk with those who come to tell me their own points of view; with those who manage the great industries and financial institutions of the country; with those who represent the farmer and the worker; and often with average citizens without high position who come to this house. And constantly I seek to look beyond the doors of the White House, beyond the officialdom of the national capital, into the hopes and fears of men and women in their homes. I have travelled the country over many times. My friends, my enemies, my daily mail bring to me reports of what you are thinking and hoping. I want to be sure that neither battles nor burdens of office shall ever blind me to an intimate knowledge of the way the American people want to live and the simple purposes for which they put me here.

In these great problems of government I try not to forget that what really counts at the bottom of it all is that the men and women willing to work can have a decent job to take care of themselves and their homes and their children adequately; that the farmer, the factory worker, the storekeeper, the gas station man, the manufacturer, the merchant—big and small—the banker who takes pride in the help that he can give to the building of his community—that all of these can be sure of a reasonable profit and safety for the savings they earn—not today nor tomorrow alone, but as far ahead as they can see.

I can hear your unspoken wonder as to where we are headed in this troubled world. I cannot expect all of the people to understand all of the people's problems; but it is my job to try to those problems.

I always try to remember that reconciling differences cannot satisfy everyone completely. Because I do not expect too much, I am not disappointed. But I know that I must never give up—that I must never let the greater interest of all the people down, merely because that might be for the moment the easiest personal way out.

I believe that we have been right in the course we have charted. To abandon our purpose of building a greater, a more stable and a more tolerant America would be to miss the tide and perhaps to miss the port. I propose to sail ahead. I feel sure that your hopes and your help are with me. For to reach a port, we must sail—sail, not lie at anchor, sail, not drift.

June 24, 1938.

Our government, happily, is a democracy. As part of the democratic process, your President is again taking an opportunity to report on the progress of national affairs, to report to the real rulers of this country—the voting public.

The Seventy-Fifth Congress, elected in November, 1936, on a platform uncompromisingly liberal, has adjourned. Barring unforeseen events, there will be no session until the new Congress, to be elected in November, assembles next January.

On the one hand, the Seventy-Fifth Congress has left many things undone.

For example, it refused to provide more businesslike machinery for running the Executive Branch of the government. The Congress also failed to meet my suggestion that it take the far-reaching steps necessary to put the railroads of the country back on their feet.

But, on the other hand, the Congress, striving to carry out the platform on which most of its members were elected, achieved more for the future good of the country than any Congress did between the end of the World War and the spring of 1933.

I mention tonight only the more important of these achievements.

(1) It improved still further our agricultural laws to give the farmer a fairer share of the national income, to preserve our soil, to provide an all-weather granary, to help the farm tenant towards independence, to find new uses for farm products, and to begin crop insurance.

(2) After many requests on my part the Congress passed a Fair Labor Standards Act, commonly called the Wages and Hours Bill. That act—applying to products in interstate commerce—ends child labor, sets a floor below wages and a ceiling over hours of labor.

Except perhaps for the Social Security Act, it is the most far-reaching, the most far-sighted program for the benefit of workers ever adopted here or in any other country. Without question it starts us toward a better standard of living and increases purchasing power to buy the products of farm and factory.

Do not let any calamity-howling executive with an income of $1,000 a day, who has been turning his employees over to the government relief rolls in order to preserve his company's undistributed reserves, tell you—using his stockholders' money to pay the postage for his personal opinions—that a wage of $11 a week is going to have a disastrous effect on all American industry. Fortunately for business as a whole, and therefore for the nation, that type of executive is a rarity with whom most business executives most heartily disagree.

(3) The Congress has provided a fact-finding Commission to find a path through the jungle of contradictory theories about the wise business practices—to find the necessary facts for any intelligent legislation on monopoly, on price-fixing and on the relationship between big business and medium-sized business and little business. Different from a great part of the world, we in America persist in our belief in individual enterprise and in the profit motive; but we realize we must continually seek improved practices to insure the continuance of reasonable profits, together with scientific progress, individual initiative, opportunities for the little fellow, fair prices, decent wages and continuing employment.

(4) The Congress has coordinated the supervision of commercial aviation and air mail by establishing a new Civil Aeronautics Authority; and it has placed all postmasters under the civil service for the first time in our national history.

(5) The Congress set up the United States Housing Authority to help finance large-scale slum clearance and provide low rent housing for the low income groups in our cities. And by improving the Federal Housing Act, the Congress made it easier for private capital to build modest homes and low rental dwellings.

(6) The Congress has properly reduced taxes on small corporate enterprises, and has made it easier for the Reconstruction Finance Corporation to make credit available to all business. I think the bankers of the country can fairly be expected to participate in loans where the government, through the Reconstruction Finance Corporation, offers to take a fair portion of the risk.

(7) The Congress has provided additional funds for the Works Progress Administration, the Public Works Administration, the Rural Electrification Administration, the Civilian Conservation Corps and other agencies, in order to take care of what we hope is a temporary additional number of

unemployed at this time and to encourage production of every kind by private enterprise.

All these things together I call our program for the national defense of our economic system. It is a program of balanced action—of moving on all fronts at once in intelligent recognition that all of our economic problems, of every group, and of every section of the country are essentially one problem.

(8) Finally, because of increasing armaments in other nations and an international situation which is definitely disturbing to all of us, the Congress has authorized important additions to the national armed defense of our shores and our people.

On another important subject the net result of a struggle in the Congress has been an important victory for the people of the United States—what might well be called a lost battle which won a war.

You will remember that on February 5, 1937, I sent a message to the Congress dealing with the real need of federal court reforms of several kinds. In one way or another, during the sessions of this Congress, the ends—the real objectives—sought in that message, have been substantially attained.

The attitude of the Supreme Court towards constitutional questions is entirely changed. Its recent decisions are eloquent testimony of a willingness to collaborate with the two other branches of government to make democracy work. The government has been granted the right to protect its interests in litigation between private parties involving the constitutionality of federal, and to appeal directly to the Supreme Court in all cases involving the constitutionality of federal statutes; and no single judge is any longer empowered to suspend a federal statute on his sole judgment as to its constitutionality. Justices of the Supreme Court may now retire at the age of seventy after ten years of service; a substantial number of additional judgeships have been created in order to expedite the trial of cases; and finally greater flexibility has been added to the federal judicial system by allowing judges to be assigned to congested districts.

Another indirect accomplishment of this Congress has been its response to the devotion of the American people to a course of sane and consistent liberalism. The Congress has understood that under modern conditions government has a continuing responsibility to meet continuing problems, and that government cannot take a holiday of a year, or a month, or even a day just because a few people are tired or frightened by the inescapable pace, fast pace, of this modern world in which we live.

Some of my opponents and some of my associates have considered that I have a mistakenly sentimental judgment as to the tenacity of purpose and the general level of intelligence of the American people.

I am still convinced that the American people, since 1932, continue to insist on two requisites of private enterprise, and the relationship of government to it. The first is a complete honesty at the top in looking after the use of other people's money, and in apportioning and paying individual and corporate taxes according to ability to pay. The second is sincere respect for the need of all people who are at the bottom, all people at the bottom who need to get work— and through work to get a really fair share of the good things of life, and a chance to save and rise.

After the election of 1936 I was told, and the Congress was told, by an increasing number of politically—and worldly—wise people that I should coast along, enjoy an easy Presidency for four years, and not take the Democratic platform too seriously. They told me that people were getting weary of reform through political effort and would no longer oppose that small minority which, in spite of its own disastrous leadership in 1929, is always eager to resume its control over the government of the United States.

Never in our lifetime has such a concerted campaign of defeatism been thrown at the heads of the President and the Senators and Congressmen as in the case of this Seventy-Fifth Congress. Never before have we had so many Copperheads—and you will remember that it was the Copperheads who, in the days of the War between the States, tried their best to make President Lincoln and his Congress give up the fight, let the nation remain split in two and return to peace—peace at any price.

This Congress has ended on the side of the people. My faith in the American people—and their faith in themselves—have been justified. I congratulate the Congress and the leadership thereof and I congratulate the American people on their own staying power.

One word about our economic situation. It makes no difference to me whether you call it a recession or a depression. In 1932 the total national income of all the people in the country had reached the low point of thirty-eight billion dollars in that year. With each succeeding year it rose. Last year, 1937, it had risen to seventy billion dollars—despite definitely worse business and agricultural prices in the last four months of last year. This year, 1938, while it is too early to do more than give an estimate, we hope that the national income will not fall below sixty billion dollars. We remember also that banking and business and farming are not falling apart like the one-hoss shay, as they did in the terrible winter of 1932-1933.

Last year mistakes were made by the leaders of private enterprise, by the leaders of labor and by the leaders of government—all three.

Last year the leaders of private enterprise pleaded for a sudden curtailment of public spending, and said they would take up the slack. But they made the mistake of increasing their inventories too fast and setting many of their prices too high for their goods to sell.

Some labor leaders goaded by decades of oppression of labor made the mistake of going too far. They were not wise in using methods which frightened many well-wishing people. They asked employers not only to bargain with them but to put up with jurisdictional disputes at the same time.

Government too made mistakes—mistakes of optimism in assuming that industry and labor would themselves make no mistakes—and government made a mistake of timing in not passing a farm bill or a wage and hour bill last year.

As a result of the lessons of all these mistakes we hope that in the future private enterprise—capital and labor alike—will operate more intelligently together, and operate in greater cooperation with their own government than they have in the past. Such cooperation on the part of both of them will be very welcome to me. Certainly at this stage there should be a united stand on the part of both of them to resist wage cuts which would further reduce purchasing power.

Today a great steel company announced a reduction in prices with a view to stimulating business recovery, and I was gratified to know that this reduction involved no wage cut. Every encouragement ought to be given to industry which accepts the large volume and high wage policy.

If this is done, it ought to result in conditions which will replace a great part of the government spending which the failure of cooperation has made necessary this year.

From March 4, 1933 down, not a single week has passed without a cry from the opposition, a small opposition, a cry "to do something, to say something, to restore confidence." There is a very articulate group of people in this country, with plenty of ability to procure publicity for their views, who have consistently refused to cooperate with the mass of the people, whether things were going well or going badly, on the ground that they required more concessions to their point of view before they would admit having what they called "confidence."

These people demanded "restoration of confidence" when the banks were closed—and demanded it again when the banks were reopened.

They demanded "restoration of confidence" when hungry people were thronging the streets—and again when the hungry people were fed and put to work.

They demanded "restoration of confidence" when droughts hit the country—and again now when our fields are laden with bounteous yields and excessive crops.

They demanded "restoration of confidence" last year when the automobile industry was running three shifts and turning out more cars than the country could buy—and again this year when the industry is trying to get rid of an automobile surplus and has shut down its factories as a result.

It is my belief that many of these people who have been crying aloud for "confidence" are beginning today to realize that that hand has been overplayed, and that they are now willing to talk cooperation instead. It is my belief that the mass of the American people do have confidence in themselves—have confidence in their ability, with the aid of government, to solve their own problems.

It is because you are not satisfied, and I am not satisfied, with the progress that we have made in finally solving our business and agricultural and social problems that I believe the great majority of you want your own government to keep on trying to solve them. In simple frankness and in simple honesty, I need all the help I can get—and I see signs of getting more help in the future from many who have fought against progress with tooth and nail.

And now following out this line of thought, I want to say a few words about the coming political primaries.

Fifty years ago party nominations were generally made in conventions—a system typified in the public imagination by a little group in a smoke-filled room who made out the party slates.

The direct primary was invented to make the nominating process a more democratic one—to give the party voters themselves a chance to pick their party candidates.

What I am going to say to you tonight does not relate to the primaries of any particular political party, but to matters of principle in all parties—Democratic, Republican, Farmer-Labor, Progressive, Socialist or any other. Let that be clearly understood.

It is my hope that everybody affiliated with any party will vote in the primaries, and that every such voter will consider the fundamental principles for which his or her party is on record. That makes for a healthy choice between the candidates of the opposing parties on Election Day in November.

An election cannot give the country a firm sense of direction if it has two or more national parties which merely have different names but are as alike in their principles and aims as peas in the same pod.

In the coming primaries in all parties, there will be many clashes between two schools of thought, generally classified as liberal and conservative. Roughly speaking, the liberal school of thought recognizes that the new conditions throughout the world call for new remedies.

Those of us in America who hold to this school of thought, insist that these new remedies can be adopted and successfully maintained in this country under our present form of government if we use government as an instrument of cooperation to provide these remedies. We believe that we can solve our problems through continuing effort, through democratic processes instead of Fascism or Communism. We are opposed to the kind of moratorium on reform which, in effect, is reaction itself.

Be it clearly understood, however, that when I use the word "liberal," I mean the believer in progressive principles of democratic, representative government and not the wild man who, in effect, leans in the direction of Communism, for that is just as dangerous as Fascism itself.

The opposing or conservative school of thought, as a general proposition, does not recognize the need for government itself to step in and take action to meet these new problems. It believes that individual initiative and private philanthropy will solve them—that we ought to repeal many of the things we have done and go back, for instance, to the old gold standard, or stop all this business of old age pensions and unemployment insurance, or repeal the Securities and Exchange Act, or let monopolies thrive unchecked—return, in effect, to the kind of government that we had in the twenties.

Assuming the mental capacity of all the candidates, the important question which it seems to me the primary voter must ask is this: "To which of these general schools of thought does the candidate belong?"

As President of the United States, I am not asking the voters of the country to vote for Democrats next November as opposed to Republicans or members of any other party. Nor am I, as President, taking part in Democratic primaries.

As the head of the Democratic Party, however, charged with the responsibility of carrying out the definitely liberal declaration of principles set forth in the 1936 Democratic platform, I feel that I have every right to speak in those few instances where there may be a clear-cut issue between candidates for a Democratic nomination involving these principles, or involving a clear misuse of my own name.

Do not misunderstand me. I certainly would not indicate a preference in a state primary merely because a candidate, otherwise liberal in outlook, had conscientiously differed with me on any single issue. I should be far more concerned about the general attitude of a candidate towards present day problems and his own inward desire to get practical needs attended to in a practical way. We all know that progress may be blocked by outspoken reactionaries, and also by those who say "yes" to a progressive objective, but who always find some reason to oppose any special specific proposal to gain that objective. I call that type of candidate a "yes, but" fellow.

And I am concerned about the attitude of a candidate or his sponsors with respect to the rights of American citizens to assemble peaceably and to express publicly their views and opinions on important social and economic issues. There can be no constitutional democracy in any community which denies to the individual his freedom to speak and worship as he wishes. The American people will not be deceived by anyone who attempts to suppress individual liberty under the pretense of patriotism.

This being a free country with freedom of expression—especially with freedom of the press—there will be a lot of mean blows struck between now and Election Day. By "blows" I mean misrepresentation, personal attack and appeals to prejudice. It would be a lot better, of course, if campaigns everywhere could be waged with arguments instead of with blows.

I hope the liberal candidates will confine themselves to argument and not resort to blows. In nine cases out of ten the speaker or the writer who, seeking to influence public opinion, descends from calm argument to unfair blows hurts himself more than his opponent.

The Chinese have a story on this—a story based on three or four thousand years of civilization: Two Chinese coolies were arguing heatedly in the midst of a crowd. A stranger expressed surprise that no blows were being struck. His Chinese friend replied: "The man who strikes first admits that his ideas have given out."

I know that neither in the summer primaries nor in the November elections will the American voters fail to spot the candidate whose ideas have given out.

September 3, 1939.

My Fellow Americans and My Friends:

Tonight my single duty is to speak to the whole of America.

Until four-thirty this morning I had hoped against hope that some miracle would prevent a devastating war in Europe and bring to an end the invasion of Poland by Germany.

For four long years a succession of actual wars and constant crises have shaken the entire world and have threatened in each case to bring on the gigantic conflict which is today unhappily a fact.

It is right that I should recall to your minds the consistent and at time successful efforts of your government in these crises to throw the full weight of the United States into the cause of peace. In spite of spreading wars I think that we have every right and every reason to maintain as a national policy the fundamental moralities, the teachings of religion and the continuation of efforts to restore peace—for some day, though the time may be distant, we can be of even greater help to a crippled humanity.

It is right, too, to point out that the unfortunate events of these recent years have, without question, been based on the use of force and the threat of force. And it seems to me clear, even at the outbreak of this great war, that the influence of America should be consistent in seeking for humanity a final peace which will eliminate, as far as it is possible to do so, the continued use of force between nations.

It is, of course, impossible to predict the future. I have my constant stream of information from American representatives and other sources throughout the world. You, the people of this country, are receiving news through your radios and your newspapers at every hour of the day.

You are, I believe, the most enlightened and the best informed people in all the world at this moment. You are subjected to no censorship of news, and I want to add that your government has no information which it withholds or which it has any thought of withholding from you.

At the same time, as I told my Press Conference on Friday, it is of the highest importance that the press and the radio use the utmost caution to discriminate between actual verified fact on the one hand, and mere rumor on the other.

I can add to that by saying that I hope the people of this country will also discriminate most carefully between news and rumor. Do not believe of necessity everything you hear or read. Check up on it first.

You must master at the outset a simple but unalterable fact in modern foreign relations between nations. When peace has been broken anywhere, the peace of all countries everywhere is in danger.

It is easy for you and for me to shrug our shoulders and to say that conflicts taking place thousands of miles from the continental United States, and, indeed, thousands of miles from the whole American Hemisphere, do not seriously affect the Americas—and that all the United States has to do is to ignore them and go about its own business. Passionately though we may desire detachment, we are forced to realize that every word that comes through the air, every ship that sails the sea, every battle that is fought does affect the American future.

Let no man or woman thoughtlessly or falsely talk of America sending its armies to European fields. At this moment there is being prepared a proclamation of American neutrality. This would have been done even if there had been no neutrality statute on the books, for this proclamation is in accordance with international law and in accordance with American policy.

This will be followed by a Proclamation required by the existing Neutrality Act. And I trust that in the days to come our neutrality can be made a true neutrality.

It is of the utmost importance that the people of this country, with the best information in the world, think things through. The most dangerous enemies of American peace are those who, without well-rounded information on the whole broad subject of the past, the present and the future, undertake to speak with assumed authority, to talk in terms of glittering generalities, to give to the nation assurances or prophecies which are of little present or future value.

I myself cannot and do not prophesy the course of events abroad—and the reason is that because I have of necessity such a complete picture of what is going on in every part of the world, that I do not dare to do so. And the other reason is that I think it is honest for me to be honest with the people of the United States.

I cannot prophesy the immediate economic effect of this new war on our nation, but I do say that no American has the moral right to profiteer at the expense either of his fellow citizens or of the men, the women and the children who are living and dying in the midst of war in Europe.

Some things we do know. Most of us in the United States believe in spiritual values. Most of us, regardless of what church we belong to, believe in the spirit of the New Testament—a great teaching which opposes itself to the use of force, of armed force, of marching armies and falling bombs. The overwhelming masses of our people seek peace—peace at home, and the kind of peace in other lands which will not jeopardize our peace at home.

We have certain ideas and certain ideals of national safety and we must act to preserve that safety today and to preserve the safety of our children in future years.

That safety is and will be bound up with the safety of the Western Hemisphere and of the seas adjacent thereto. We seek to keep war from our own firesides by keeping war from coming to the Americas. For that we have historic precedent that goes back to the days of the administration of President George Washington. It is serious enough and tragic enough to every American family in every state in the Union to live in a world that is torn by wars on other continents. Those wars today affect every American home. It is our national duty to use every effort to keep them out of the Americas.

And at this time let me make the simple plea that partisanship and selfishness be adjourned; and that national unity be the thought that underlies all others.

This nation will remain a neutral nation, but I cannot ask that every American remain neutral in thought as well. Even a neutral has a right to take account of facts. Even a neutral cannot be asked to close his mind or his conscience.

I have said not once but many times that I have seen war and that I hate war. I say that again and again.

I hope the United States will keep out of this war. I believe that it will. And I give you assurance and reassurance that every effort of your government will be directed toward that end.

As long as it remains within my power to prevent, there will be no blackout of peace in the United States.

May 26, 1940.

My Friends:

At this moment of sadness throughout most of the world, I want to talk with you about a number of subjects that directly affect the future of the United States. We are shocked by the almost incredible eyewitness stories that come to us, stories of what is happening at this moment to the civilian populations of Norway and Holland and Belgium and Luxembourg and France.

I think it is right on this Sabbath evening that I should say a word in behalf of women and children and old men who need help—immediate help in their present distress—help from us across the seas, help from us who are still free to give it.

Tonight over the once peaceful roads of Belgium and France millions are now moving, running from their homes to escape bombs and shells and fire and machine gunning, without shelter, and almost wholly without food. They stumble on, knowing not where the end of the road will be. I speak to you of these people because each one of you that is listening to me tonight has a way of helping them. The American Red Cross, that represents each of us, is rushing food and clothing and medical supplies to these destitute civilian millions. Please—I beg you—please give according to your means to your nearest Red Cross chapter, give as generously as you can. I ask this in the name of our common humanity.

Let us sit down together again, you and I, to consider our own pressing problems that confront us.

There are many among us who in the past closed their eyes to events abroad—because they believed in utter good faith what some of their fellow Americans told them—that what was taking place in Europe was none of our business; that no matter what happened over there, the United States could always pursue its peaceful and unique course in the world.

There are many among us who closed their eyes, from lack of interest or lack of knowledge; honestly and sincerely thinking that the many hundreds of miles of salt water made the American Hemisphere so remote that the people of North and Central and South America could go on living in the midst of their vast resources without reference to, or danger from, other Continents of the world.

There are some among us who were persuaded by minority groups that we could maintain our physical safety by retiring within our continental boundaries—the Atlantic on the east, the Pacific on the west, Canada on the north and Mexico on the south. I illustrated the futility—the impossibility—of that idea in my message to the Congress last week. Obviously, a defense policy based on that is merely to invite future attack.

And, finally, there are a few among us who have deliberately and consciously closed their eyes because they were determined to be opposed to their government, its foreign policy and every other policy, to be partisan, and to believe that anything that the government did was wholly wrong.

To those who have closed their eyes for any of these many reasons, to those who would not admit the possibility of the approaching storm—to all of them the past two weeks have meant the shattering of many illusions.

They have lost the illusion that we are remote and isolated and, therefore, secure against the dangers from which no other land is free.

In some quarters, with this rude awakening has come fear, fear bordering on panic. It is said that we are defenseless. It is whispered by some that, only by abandoning our freedom, our ideals, our way of life, can we build our defenses adequately, can we match the strength of the aggressors.

I did not share those illusions. I do not share these fears.

Today we are now more realistic. But let us not be calamity-howlers and discount our strength. Let us have done with both fears and illusions. On this Sabbath evening, in our homes in the midst of our American families, let us calmly consider what we have done and what we must do.

In the past two or three weeks all kinds of stories have been handed out to the American public about our lack of preparedness. It has even been charged that the money we have spent on our military and naval forces during the last few years has gone down the rat-hole. I think that it is a matter of fairness to the nation that you hear the facts.

Yes, we have spent large sums of money on the national defense. This money has been used to make our Army and Navy today the largest, the best equipped, and the best trained peace-time military establishment in the whole history of this country.

Let me tell you just a few of the many things accomplished during the past few years.

I do not propose to go into every detail. It is a known fact, however, that in 1933, when this administration came into office, the United States Navy had fallen in standing among the navies of the world, in power of ships and in efficiency, to a relatively low ebb. The relative fighting power on the Navy had been greatly diminished by failure to replace ships and equipment, which had become out-of-date.

But between 1933 and this year, 1940—seven fiscal years—your government will have spent one billion, four hundred eighty-seven million dollars more than it spent on the Navy during the seven years that preceded 1933.

What did we get for this money?

The fighting personnel of the Navy rose from 79,000 to 145,000.

During this period 215 ships for the fighting fleet have been laid down or commissioned, practically seven times the number in the preceding seven-year period.

Of these 215 ships we have commissioned: 12 cruisers; 63 destroyers; 26 submarines; 3 aircraft carriers; 2 gunboats; 7 auxiliaries and many smaller craft. And among the many ships now being built and paid for as we build them are 8 new battleships.

Ship construction, of course, costs millions of dollars—more in the United States than anywhere else in the world; but it is a fact that we cannot have adequate navy defense for all American waters without ships—ships that sail the surface of the ocean, ships that move under the surface and ships that move through the air. And, speaking of airplanes that work with the Navy, in 1933 we had 1,127 useful aircraft and today we have 2,892 on hand and on order. Nearly all of the old planes of 1933 have been replaced by new planes because they became obsolete or worn out.

The Navy Is far stronger today than at any peace-time period in the whole long history of the nation. In hitting power and in efficiency, I would even make the assertion that it is stronger today than it was during the World War.

The Army of the United States: In 1933 it consisted of 122,000 enlisted men. Now, in 1940, that number has been practically doubled. The Army of 1933 had been given few new implements of war since 1919, and had been compelled to draw on old reserve stocks left over from the World War.

The net result of all this was that our Army by 1933 had very greatly declined in its ratio of strength with the armies of Europe and of the Far East.

That was the situation I found.

But, since then, great changes have taken place.

Between 1933 and 1940—these past seven fiscal years—your government will have spent $1,292,000,000 more than it spent on the Army the previous seven years.

What did we get for this money?

The personnel of the Army, as I have said, has been almost doubled. And by the end of this year every existing unit of the present regular Army will be equipped with its complete requirements of modern weapons. Existing units of the national Guard will also be largely equipped with similar items.

Here are some striking examples taken from a large number:

Since 1933 we have actually purchased 5,640 airplanes, including the most modern type of long-range bombers and fast pursuit planes, though, of course, many of these which were delivered four, five, six or seven years ago have worn out through use and been scrapped.

We must remember that these planes cost money—a lot of it. For example, one modern four-engine long-range bombing plane costs $350,000; one modern interceptor pursuit plane costs $133,000; one medium bomber costs $160,000.

In 1933 we had only 355 anti-aircraft guns. We now have more than 1,700 modern anti-craft guns of all types on hand or on order. And you ought to know that a three-inch anti-aircraft gun costs $40,000 without any of the fire control equipment that goes with it.

In 1933 there were only 24 modern infantry mortars in the entire Army. We now have on hand and on order more than 1,600.

In 1933 we had only 48 modern tanks and armored cars; today we have on hand and on order 1,700. Each one of our heavier tanks costs $46,000.

There are many other items in which our progress since 1933 has been rapid. And the great proportion of this advance consists of really modern equipment.

In 1933, on the personnel side we had 1,263 Army pilots. Today the Army alone has more than 3,000 of the best fighting flyers in the world, flyers who last year flew more than one million hours in combat training. That figure does not include the hundreds of splendid pilots in the national Guard and in the organized reserves.

Within the past year the productive capacity of the aviation industry to produce military planes has been tremendously increased. In the past year the capacity more than doubled, but that capacity is still inadequate. However, the government, working with industry, is determined to increase that capacity to meet our needs. We intend to harness the efficient machinery of these manufacturers to the government's program of being able to get 50,000 planes a year.

One additional word about aircraft, about which we read so much. Recent wars, including the current war in Europe, have demonstrated beyond doubt that fighting efficiency depends on unity of command, unity of control.

In sea operations the airplane is just as much an integral part of the unity of operations as are the submarine, the destroyer and the battleship, and in land warfare the airplane is just as much a part of military operations as are the tank corps, the engineers, the artillery or the infantry itself. Therefore, the air forces should continue to be part of the Army and Navy.

In line with my request the Congress, this week, is voting the largest appropriation ever asked by the Army or the Navy in peacetime, and the equipment and training provided for them will be in addition to the figures I have given you.

The world situation may so change that it will be necessary to reappraise our program at any time. And in such case I am confident that the Congress and the Chief Executive will work in harmony as a team as they are doing today.

I will not hesitate at any moment to ask for additional funds when they are required.

In this era of swift, mechanized warfare, we all have to remember that what is modern today and up-to-date, what is efficient and practical, becomes obsolete and outworn tomorrow.

Even while the production line turns out airplanes, new airplanes are being designed on the drafting table.

Even as a cruiser slides down the launching ways, plans for improvement, plans for increased efficiency in the next model, are taking shape in the blueprints of designers.

Every day's fighting in Europe, on land, on sea, and in the air, discloses constant changes in methods of warfare. We are constantly improving and redesigning, testing new weapons, learning the lessons of the immediate war, and seeking to produce in accordance with the latest that the brains of science can conceive.

We are calling upon the resources, the efficiency and the ingenuity of the American manufacturers of war material of all kinds—airplanes and tanks and guns and ships, and all the hundreds of products that go into this material. The government of the United States itself manufactures few of the implements of war. Private industry will continue to be the source of most of this materiel, and private industry will have to be speeded up to produce it at the rate and efficiency called for by the needs of the times.

I know that private business cannot be expected to make all of the capital investment required for expansions of plants and factories and personnel which this program calls for at once. It would be unfair to expect industrial corporations or their investors to do this, when there is a chance that a change in international affairs may stop or curtail future orders a year or two hence.

Therefore, the government of the United States stands ready to advance the necessary money to help provide for the enlargement of factories, the establishment of new plants, the employment of thousands of necessary workers, the development of new sources of supply for the hundreds of raw materials required, the development of quick mass transportation of supplies.

And the details of all of this are now being worked out in Washington, day and night.

We are calling on men now engaged in private industry to help us in carrying out this program and you will hear more of this in detail in the next few days.

This does not mean that the men we call upon will be engaged in the actual production of this materiel. That will still have to be carried on in the plants and factories throughout the land. Private industry will have the responsibility of providing the best, speediest and most efficient mass production of which it is capable. The functions of the businessmen whose assistance we are calling upon will be to coordinate this program—to see to it that all of the plants continue to operate at maximum speed and efficiency.

Patriotic Americans of proven merit and of unquestioned ability in their special fields are coming to Washington to help the government with their training, their experience and their capability.

It is our purpose not only to speed up production but to increase the total facilities of the nation in such a way that they can be further enlarged to meet emergencies of the future.

But as this program proceeds there are several things we must continue to watch and safeguard, things which are just as important to the sound defense of a nation as physical armament itself. While our Navy and our airplanes and our guns and our ships may be our first line of defense, it is still clear that way down at the bottom, underlying them all, giving them their strength, sustenance and power, are the spirit and morale of a free people.

For that reason, we must make sure, in all that we do, that there be no breakdown or cancellation of any of the great social gains which we have made in these past years. We have carried on an offensive on a broad front against social and economic inequalities and abuses which had made our society weak. That offensive should not now be broken down by the pincers movement of those who would use the present needs of physical military defense to destroy it.

There is nothing in our present emergency to justify making the workers of our nation toil for longer hours than now limited by statute. As more orders come in and as more work has to be done, tens of thousands of people, who are now unemployed, will, I believe, receive employment.

There is nothing in our present emergency to justify a lowering of the standards of employment. Minimum wages should not be reduced. It is my hope, indeed, that the new speed-up of production will cause many businesses which now pay below the minimum standards to bring their wages up.

There is nothing in our present emergency to justify a breaking down of old age pensions or of unemployment insurance. I would rather see the systems extended to other groups who do not now enjoy them.

There is nothing in our present emergency to justify a retreat from any of our social objectives—from conservation of natural resources, assistance to agriculture, housing, and help to the underprivileged.

Conversely, however, I am sure that responsible leaders will not permit some specialized group, which represents a minority of the total employees of a plant or an industry, to break up the continuity of employment of the majority of the employees. Let us remember that the policy and the laws that provide for collective bargaining are still in force. I can assure you that labor will be adequately represented in Washington in the carrying out of this program of defense.

Also, our present emergency and a common sense of decency make it imperative that no new group of war millionaires shall come into being in this nation as a result of the struggles abroad. The American people will not relish the idea of any American citizen growing rich and fat in an emergency of blood and slaughter and human suffering.

And, last of all, this emergency demands that the consumers of America be protected so that our general cost of living can be maintained at a reasonable level. We ought to avoid the spiral processes of the World War, the rising spiral of costs of all kinds. The soundest policy is for every employer in the country to help give useful employment to the millions who are unemployed. By giving to those millions an increased purchasing power, the prosperity of the whole nation will rise to a much higher level.

Today's threat to our national security is not a matter of military weapons alone. We know of new methods of attack.

The Trojan Horse. The Fifth Column that betrays a nation unprepared for treachery.

Spies, saboteurs and traitors are the actors in this new strategy. With all of these we must and will deal vigorously.

But there is an added technique for weakening a nation at its very roots, for disrupting the entire pattern of life of a people. And it is important that we understand it.

The method is simple. It is, first, a dissemination of discord. A group—not too large—a group that may be sectional or racial or political—is encouraged to exploit its prejudices through false slogans and emotional appeals. The aim of those who deliberately egg on these groups is to create confusion of counsel, public indecision, political paralysis and eventually, a state of panic.

Sound national policies come to be viewed with a new and unreasoning skepticism, not through the wholesome political debates of honest and free men, but through the clever schemes of foreign agents.

As a result of these new techniques, armament programs may be dangerously delayed. Singleness of national purpose may be undermined. Men can lose confidence in each other, and therefore lose confidence in the efficacy of their own united action. Faith and courage can yield to doubt and fear. The unity of the State can be so sapped that its strength is destroyed.

All this is no idle dream. It has happened time after time, in nation after nation, during the last two years. Fortunately, American men and women are not easy dupes. Campaigns of group hatred or class struggle have never made much headway among us, and are not making headway now. But new forces are being unleashed, deliberately planned propaganda to divide and weaken us in the face of danger as other nations have been weakened before.

These dividing forces are undiluted poison. They must not be allowed to spread in the New World as they have in the Old. Our morale and our mental defenses must be raised up as never before against those who would cast a smokescreen across our vision.

The development of our defense program makes it essential that each and every one of us, men and women, feel that we have some contribution to make toward the security of our nation.

At this time, when the world—and the world includes our own American Hemisphere—when the world is threatened by forces of destruction, it is my resolve and yours to build up our armed defenses.

We shall build them to whatever heights the future may require.

We shall rebuild them swiftly, as the methods of warfare swiftly change.

For more than three centuries we Americans have been building on this continent a free society, a society in which the promise of the human spirit may find fulfillment. Commingled here are the blood and genius of all the peoples of the world who have sought this promise.

We have built well. We are continuing our efforts to bring the blessings of a free society, of a free and productive economic system, to every family in the land. This is the promise of America.

It is this that we must continue to build—this that we must continue to defend.

It is the task of our generation, yours and mine. But we build and defend not for our generation alone. We defend the foundations laid down by our fathers. We build a life for generations yet unborn. We defend and we build a way of life, not for America alone, but for all mankind. Ours is a high duty, a noble task.

Day and night I pray for the restoration of peace in this mad world of ours. It is not necessary that I, the President, ask the American people to pray in behalf of such a cause—for I know you are praying with me.

I am certain that out of the hearts of every man, woman and child in this land, in every waking minute, a supplication goes up to Almighty God; that all of us beg that suffering and starving, that death and destruction may end—and that peace may return to the world. In common affection for all mankind, your prayers join with mine—that God will heal the wounds and the hearts of humanity.

September 11, 1941.

My Fellow Americans:

The Navy Department of the United States has reported to me that on the morning of September fourth the United States destroyer GREER, proceeding in full daylight towards Iceland, had reached a point southeast of Greenland. She was carrying American mail to Iceland. She was flying the American flag. Her identity as an American ship was unmistakable.

She was then and there attacked by a submarine. Germany admits that it was a German submarine. The submarine deliberately fired a torpedo at the GREER, followed later by another torpedo attack. In spite of what Hitler's propaganda bureau has invented, and in spite of what any American obstructionist organization may prefer to believe, I tell you the blunt fact that the German submarine fired first upon this American destroyer without warning, and with deliberate design to sink her.

Our destroyer, at the time, was in waters which the government of the United States had declared to be waters of self-defense—surrounding outposts of American protection in the Atlantic.

In the North of the Atlantic, outposts have been established by us in Iceland, in Greenland, in Labrador and in Newfoundland. Through these waters there pass many ships of many flags. They bear food and other supplies to civilians; and they bear material of war, for which the people of the United States are spending billions of dollars, and which, by Congressional action, they have declared to be essential for the defense of our own land.

The United States destroyer, when attacked, was proceeding on a legitimate mission.

If the destroyer was visible to the submarine when the torpedo was fired, then the attack was a deliberate attempt by the Nazis to sink a clearly identified American warship. On the other hand, if the submarine was beneath the surface of the sea and, with the aid of its listening devices, fired in the direction of the sound of the American destroyer without even taking the trouble to learn its identity—as the official German communique would indicate—then the attack was even more outrageous. For it indicates a policy of indiscriminate violence against any vessel sailing the seas—belligerent or non-belligerent.

This was piracy—piracy legally and morally. It was not the first nor the last act of piracy which the Nazi government has committed against the American flag in this war. For attack has followed attack.

A few months ago an American flag merchant ship, the ROBIN MOOR, was sunk by a Nazi submarine in the middle of the South Atlantic, under circumstances violating long-established international law and violating every principle of humanity. The passengers and the crew were forced into open boats hundreds of miles from land, in direct violation of international agreements signed by nearly all nations including the government of Germany. No apology, no allegation of mistake, no offer of reparations has come from the Nazi government.

In July, 1941, nearly two months ago an American battleship in North American waters was followed by a submarine which for a long time sought to maneuver itself into a position of attack upon the battleship. The periscope of the submarine was clearly seen. No British or American submarines were within hundreds of miles of this spot at the time, so the nationality of the submarine is clear.

Five days ago a United States Navy ship on patrol picked up three survivors of an American-owned ship operating under the flag of our sister Republic of Panama—the S. S. SESSA. On August seventeenth, she had been first torpedoed without warning, and then shelled, near Greenland, while carrying civilian supplies to Iceland. It is feared that the other members of her crew have been drowned. In view of the established presence of German submarines in this vicinity, there can be no reasonable doubt as to the identity of the flag of the attacker.

Five days ago, another United states merchant ship, the STEEL SEAFARER, was sunk by a German aircraft in the Red Sea two hundred and twenty miles south of Suez. She was bound for an Egyptian port.

So four of the vessels sunk or attacked flew the American flag and were clearly identifiable. Two of these ships were warships of the American Navy. In the fifth case, the vessel sunk clearly carried the flag of our sister Republic of Panama.

In the face of all this, we Americans are keeping our feet on the ground. Our type of democratic civilization has outgrown the thought of feeling compelled to fight some other nation by reason of any single piratical attack on one of our ships. We are not becoming hysterical or losing our sense of proportion. Therefore, what I am thinking and saying tonight does not relate to any isolated episode.

Instead, we Americans are taking a long-range point of view in regard certain fundamentals and to a series of events on land and on sea which must be considered as a whole—as a part of a world pattern.

It would be unworthy of a great nation to exaggerate an isolated incident, or to become inflamed by some one act of violence. But it would be inexcusable folly to minimize such incidents in the face of evidence which makes it clear that the incident is not isolated, but is part of a general plan.

The important truth is that these acts of international lawlessness are a manifestation of a design which has been made clear to the American people for a long time. It is the Nazi design to abolish the freedom of the seas, and to acquire absolute control and domination of these seas for themselves.

For with control of the seas in their own hands, the way can obviously become clear for their next step—domination of the United States—domination of the Western Hemisphere by force of arms. Under Nazi control of the seas, no merchant ship of the United States or of any other American Republic would be free to carry on any peaceful commerce, except by the condescending grace of this foreign and tyrannical power. The Atlantic Ocean which has been, and which should always be, a free and friendly highway for us would then become a deadly menace to the commerce of the United States, to the coasts of the United States, and even to the inland cities of the United States.

The Hitler government, in defiance of the laws of the sea, in defiance of the recognized rights of all other nations, has presumed to declare, on paper, that great areas of the seas—even including a vast expanse lying in the Western Hemisphere—are to be closed, and that no ships may enter them for any purpose, except at peril of being sunk. Actually they are sinking ships at will and without warning in widely separated areas both within and far outside of these far-flung pretended zones.

This Nazi attempt to seize control of the oceans is but a counterpart of the Nazi plots now being carried on throughout the Western Hemisphere—all designed toward the same end. For Hitler's advance guards—not only his avowed agents but also his dupes among us—have sought to make ready for him footholds, and bridgeheads in the New World, to be used as soon as he has gained control of the oceans.

His intrigues, his plots, his machinations, his sabotage in this New World are all known to the government of the United States. Conspiracy has followed conspiracy.

For example, last year a plot to seize the government of Uruguay was smashed by the prompt action of that country, which was supported in full by her American neighbors. A like plot was then hatching in Argentina, and that government has carefully and wisely blocked it at every point. More recently, an endeavor was made to subvert the government of Bolivia. And within the past few weeks the discovery was made of secret air-landing fields in Colombia, within easy range of the Panama Canal. I could multiply instance upon instance.

To be ultimately successful in world mastery, Hitler knows that he must get control of the seas. He must first destroy the bridge of ships which we are building across the Atlantic and over which we shall continue to roll the implements of war to help destroy him, to destroy all his works in the end. He must wipe out our patrol on sea and in the air if he is to do it. He must silence the British Navy.

I think it must be explained over and over again to people who like to think of the United States Navy as an invincible protection, that this can be true only if the British Navy survives. And that, my friends, is simple arithmetic.

For if the world outside of the Americas falls under Axis domination, the shipbuilding facilities which the Axis powers would then possess in all of Europe, in the British Isles and in the Far East would be much greater than all the shipbuilding facilities and potentialities of all of the Americas—not only greater, but two or three times greater—enough to win. Even if the United States threw all its resources into such a situation, seeking to double and even redouble the size of our Navy, the Axis powers, in control of the rest of the world, would have the manpower and the physical resources to outbuild us several times over.

It is time for all Americans, Americans of all the Americas to stop being deluded by the romantic notion that the Americas can go on living happily and peacefully in a Nazi-dominated world.

Generation after generation, America has battled for the general policy of the freedom of the seas. And that policy is a very simple one—but a basic, a fundamental one. It means that no nation has the right to make the broad oceans of the world at great distances from the actual theatre of land war, unsafe for the commerce of others.

That has been our policy, proved time and time again, in all of our history.

Our policy has applied from the earliest days of the Republic—and still applies—not merely to the Atlantic but to the Pacific and to all other oceans as well.

Unrestricted submarine warfare in 1941 constitutes a defiance—an act of aggression—against that historic American policy.

It is now clear that Hitler has begun his campaign to control the seas by ruthless force and by wiping out every vestige of international law, every vestige of humanity.

His intention has been made clear. The American people can have no further illusions about it.

No tender whisperings of appeasers that Hitler is not interested in the Western Hemisphere, no soporific lullabies that a wide ocean protects us from him—can long have any effect on the hard-headed, far-sighted and realistic American people.

Because of these episodes, because of the movements and operations of German warships, and because of the clear, repeated proof that the present government of Germany has no respect for treaties or for international law, that it has no decent attitude toward neutral nations or human life—we Americans are now face to face not with abstract theories but with cruel, relentless facts.

This attack on the GREER was no localized military operation in the North Atlantic. This was no mere episode in a struggle between two nations. This was one determined step towards creating a permanent world system based on force, on terror and on murder.

And I am sure that even now the Nazis are waiting to see whether the United States will by silence give them the green light to go ahead on this path of destruction.

The Nazi danger to our Western world has long ceased to be a mere possibility. The danger is here now—not only from a military enemy but from an enemy of all law, all liberty, all morality, all religion.

There has now come a time when you and I must see the cold inexorable necessity of saying to these inhuman, unrestrained seekers of world conquest and permanent world domination by the sword: "You seek to throw our children and our children's children into your form of terrorism and slavery. You have now attacked our own safety. You shall go no further."

Normal practices of diplomacy—note writing—are of no possible use in dealing with international outlaws who sink our ships and kill our citizens.

One peaceful nation after another has met disaster because each refused to look the Nazi danger squarely in the eye until it had actually had them by the throat.

The United States will not make that fatal mistake.

No act of violence, no act of intimidation will keep us from maintaining intact two bulwarks of American defense: First, our line of supply of material to the enemies of Hitler; and second, the freedom of our shipping on the high seas.

No matter what it takes, no matter what it costs, we will keep open the line of legitimate commerce in these defensive water.

We have sought no shooting war with Hitler. We do not seek it now. But neither do we want peace so much, that we are willing to pay for it by permitting him to attack our naval and merchant ships while they are on legitimate business.

I assume that the German leaders are not deeply concerned, tonight or any other time, by what we Americans or the American government say or publish about them. We cannot bring about the downfall of Nazism by the use of long-range invective.

But when you see a rattlesnake poised to strike, you do not wait until he has struck before you crush him.

These Nazi submarines and raiders are the rattlesnakes of the Atlantic. They are a menace to the free pathways of the high seas. They are a challenge to our own sovereignty. They hammer at our most precious rights when they attack ships of the American flag—symbols of our independence, our freedom, our very life.

It is clear to all Americans that the time has come when the Americas themselves must now be defended. A continuation of attacks in our own waters or in waters that could be used for further and greater attacks on us, will inevitably weaken our American ability to repel Hitlerism.

Do not let us be hair-splitters. Let us not ask ourselves whether the Americas should begin to defend themselves after the first attack, or the fifth attack, or the tenth attack, or the twentieth attack.

The time for active defense is now.

Do not let us split hairs. Let us not say: "We will only defend ourselves if the torpedo succeeds in getting home, or if the crew and the passengers are drowned".

This is the time for prevention of attack.

If submarines or raiders attack in distant waters, they can attack equally well within sight of our own shores. Their very presence in any waters which America deems vital to its defense constitutes an attack.

In the waters which we deem necessary for our defense, American naval vessels and American planes will no longer wait until Axis submarines lurking under the water, or Axis raiders on the surface of the sea, strike their deadly blow—first.

Upon our naval and air patrol—now operating in large number over a vast expanse of the Atlantic Ocean—falls the duty of maintaining the American policy of freedom of the seas—now. That means, very simply, very clearly, that our patrolling vessels and planes will protect all merchant ships—not only American ships but ships of any flag—engaged in commerce in our defensive waters. They will protect them from submarines; they will protect them from surface raiders.

This situation is not new. The second President of the United States, John Adams, ordered the United States Navy to clean out European privateers and European ships of war which were infesting the Caribbean and South American waters, destroying American commerce.

The third President of the United States, Thomas Jefferson, ordered the United States Navy to end the attacks being made upon American and other ships by the corsairs of the nations of North Africa.

My obligation as President is historic; it is clear. It is inescapable.

It is no act of war on our part when we decide to protect the seas that are vital to American defense. The aggression is not ours. Ours is solely defense.

But let this warning be clear. From now on, if German or Italian vessels of war enter the waters, the protection of which is necessary for American defense, they do so at their own peril.

The orders which I have given as Commander-in-Chief of the United States Army and Navy are to carry out that policy—at once.

The sole responsibility rests upon Germany. There will be no shooting unless Germany continues to seek it.

That is my obvious duty in this crisis. That is the clear right of this sovereign nation. This is the only step possible, if we would keep tight the wall of defense which we are pledged to maintain around this Western Hemisphere.

I have no illusions about the gravity of this step. I have not taken it hurriedly or lightly. It is the result of months and months of constant thought and anxiety and prayer. In the protection of your nation and mine it cannot be avoided.

The American people have faced other grave crises in their history—with American courage, and with American resolution. They will do no less today.

They know the actualities of the attacks upon us. They know the necessities of a bold defense against these attacks. They know that the times call for clear heads and fearless hearts.

And with that inner strength that comes to a free people conscious of their duty, and conscious of the righteousness of what they do, they will—with Divine help and guidance—stand their ground against this latest assault upon their democracy, their sovereignty, and their freedom.

December 9, 1941.

My Fellow Americans:

The sudden criminal attacks perpetrated by the Japanese in the Pacific provide the climax of a decade of international immorality.

Powerful and resourceful gangsters have banded together to make war upon the whole human race. Their challenge has now been flung at the United States of America. The Japanese have treacherously violated the long-standing peace between us. Many American soldiers and sailors have been killed by enemy action. American ships have been sunk; American airplanes have been destroyed.

The Congress and the people of the United States have accepted that challenge.

Together with other free peoples, we are now fighting to maintain our right to live among our world neighbors in freedom, in common decency, without fear of assault.

I have prepared the full record of our past relations with Japan, and it will be submitted to the Congress. It begins with the visit of Commodore Perry to Japan eighty-eight years ago. It ends with the visit of two Japanese emissaries to the Secretary of State last Sunday, an hour after Japanese forces had loosed their bombs and machine guns against our flag, our forces and our citizens.

I can say with utmost confidence that no Americans, today or a thousand years hence, need feel anything but pride in our patience and in our efforts through all the years toward achieving a peace in the Pacific which would be fair and honorable to every nation, large or small. And no honest person, today or a thousand years hence, will be able to suppress a sense of indignation and horror at the treachery committed by the military dictators of Japan, under the very shadow of the flag of peace borne by their special envoys in our midst.

The course that Japan has followed for the past ten years in Asia has paralleled the course of Hitler and Mussolini in Europe and in Africa. Today, it has become far more than a parallel. It is actual collaboration so well calculated that all the continents of the world, and all the oceans, are now considered by the Axis strategists as one gigantic battlefield.

In 1931, ten years ago, Japan invaded Manchukuo—without warning.

In 1935, Italy invaded Ethiopia—without warning. In 1938, Hitler occupied Austria—without warning.

In 1939, Hitler invaded Czechoslovakia—without warning.

Later in '39, Hitler invaded Poland—without warning.

In 1940, Hitler invaded Norway, Denmark, the Netherlands, Belgium and Luxembourg—without warning.

In 1940, Italy attacked France and later Greece—without warning.

And this year, in 1941, the Axis Powers attacked Yugoslavia and Greece and they dominated the Balkans—without warning.

In 1941, also, Hitler invaded Russia—without warning.

And now Japan has attacked Malaya and Thailand—and the United States—without warning.

It is all of one pattern.

We are now in this war. We are all in it—all the way. Every single man, woman and child is a partner in the most tremendous undertaking of our American history. We must share together the bad news and the good news, the defeats and the victories—the changing fortunes of war.

So far, the news has been all bad. We have suffered a serious setback in Hawaii. Our forces in the Philippines, which include the brave people of that Commonwealth, are taking punishment, but are defending themselves vigorously. The reports from Guam and Wake and Midway Islands are still confused, but we must be prepared for the announcement that all these three outposts have been seized.

The casualty lists of these first few days will undoubtedly be large. I deeply feel the anxiety of all of the families of the men in our armed forces and the relatives of people in cities which have been bombed. I can only give them my solemn promise that they will get news just as quickly as possible.

This government will put its trust in the stamina of the American people, and will give the facts to the public just as soon as two conditions have been fulfilled: first, that the information has been definitely and officially confirmed; and, second, that the release of the information at the time it is received will not prove valuable to the enemy directly or indirectly.

Most earnestly I urge my countrymen to reject all rumors. These ugly little hints of complete disaster fly thick and fast in wartime. They have to be examined and appraised.

As an example, I can tell you frankly that until further surveys are made, I have not sufficient information to state the exact damage which has been done to our naval vessels at Pearl Harbor. Admittedly the damage is serious. But no one can say how serious, until we know how much of this damage can be repaired and how quickly the necessary repairs can be made.

I cite as another example a statement made on Sunday night that a Japanese carrier had been located and sunk off the Canal Zone. And when you hear statements that are attributed to what they call "an authoritative source," you can be reasonably sure from now on that under these war circumstances the "authoritative source" is not any person in authority.

Many rumors and reports which we now hear originate with enemy sources. For instance, today the Japanese are claiming that as a result of their one action against Hawaii they hare gained naval supremacy in the Pacific. This is an old trick of propaganda which has been used innumerable times by the Nazis. The purposes of such fantastic claims are, of course, to spread fear and confusion among us, and to goad us into revealing military information which our enemies are desperately anxious to obtain.

Our government will not be caught in this obvious trap—and neither will the people of the United States.

It must be remembered by each and every one of us that our free and rapid communication these days must be greatly restricted in wartime. It is not possible to receive full and speedy and accurate reports front distant areas of combat. This is particularly true where naval operations are concerned. For in these days of the marvels of the radio it is often impossible for the Commanders of various units to report their activities by radio at all, for the very simple reason that this information would become available to the enemy and would disclose their position and their plan of defense or attack.

Of necessity there will be delays in officially confirming or denying reports of operations, but we will not hide facts from the country if we know the facts and if the enemy will not be aided by their disclosure.

To all newspapers and radio stations—all those who reach the eyes and ears of the American people—I say this: You have a most grave responsibility to the nation now and for the duration of this war.

If you feel that your government is not disclosing enough of the truth, you have every right to say so. But in the absence of all the facts, as revealed by official sources, you have no right in the ethics of patriotism to deal out unconfirmed reports in such a way as to make people believe that they are gospel truth.

Every citizen, in every walk of life, shares this same responsibility. The lives of our soldiers and sailors—the whole future of this nation—depend upon the manner in which each and every one of us fulfills his obligation to our country.

Now a word about the recent past—and the future. A year and a half has elapsed since the fall of France, when the whole world first realized the mechanized might which the Axis nations had been building up for so many years. America has used that year and a half to great advantage. Knowing that the attack might reach us in all too short a time, we immediately began greatly to increase our industrial strength and our capacity to meet the demands of modern warfare.

Precious months were gained by sending vast quantities of our war material to the nations of the world still able to resist Axis aggression. Our policy rested on the fundamental truth that the defense of any country resisting Hitler or Japan was in the long run the defense of our own country. That policy has been justified. It has given us time, invaluable time, to build our American assembly lines of production.

Assembly lines are now in operation. Others are being rushed to completion. A steady stream of tanks and planes, of guns and ships and shells and equipment—that is what these eighteen months have given us.

But it is all only a beginning of what still has to be done. We must be set to face a long war against crafty and powerful bandits. The attack at Pearl Harbor can be repeated at any one of many points, points in both oceans and along both our coast lines and against all the rest of the Hemisphere.

It will not only be a long war, it will be a hard war. That is the basis on which we now lay all our plans. That is the yardstick by which we measure what we shall need and demand; money, materials, doubled and quadrupled production—ever-increasing. The production must be not only for our own Army and Navy and air forces. It must reinforce the other armies and navies and air forces fighting the Nazis and the war lords of Japan throughout the Americas and throughout the world.

I have been working today on the subject of production. Your government has decided on two broad policies.

The first is to speed up all existing production by working on a seven day week basis in every war industry, including the production of essential raw materials.

The second policy, now being put into form, is to rush additions to the capacity of production by building more new plants, by adding to old plants, and by using the many smaller plants for war needs.

Over the hard road of the past months, we have at times met obstacles and difficulties, divisions and disputes, indifference and callousness. That is now all past—and, I am sure, forgotten.

The fact is that the country now has an organization in Washington built around men and women who are recognized experts in their own fields. I think the country knows that the people who are actually responsible in each and every one of these many fields are pulling together with a teamwork that has never before been excelled.

On the road ahead there lies hard work—grueling work—day and night, every hour and every minute.

I was about to add that ahead there lies sacrifice for all of us.

But it is not correct to use that word. The United States does not consider it a sacrifice to do all one can, to give one's best to our nation, when the nation is fighting for its existence and its future life.

It is not a sacrifice for any man, old or young, to be in the Army or the Navy of the United States. Rather it is a privilege.

It is not a sacrifice for the industrialist or the wage earner, the farmer or the shopkeeper, the trainman or the doctor, to pay more taxes, to buy more bonds, to forego extra profits, to work longer or harder at the task for which he is best fitted. Rather it is a privilege.

It is not a sacrifice to do without many things to which we are accustomed if the national defense calls for doing without.

A review this morning leads me to the conclusion that at present we shall not have to curtail the normal use of articles of food. There is enough food today for all of us and enough left over to send to those who are fighting on the same side with us.

But there will be a clear and definite shortage of metals for many kinds of civilian use, for the very good reason that in our increased program we shall need for war purposes more than half of that portion of the principal metals which during the past year have gone into articles for civilian use. Yes, we shall have to give up many things entirely.

And I am sure that the people in every part of the nation are prepared in their individual living to win this war. I am sure that they will cheerfully help to pay a large part of its financial cost while it goes on. I am sure they will cheerfully give up those material things that they are asked to give up.

And I am sure that they will retain all those great spiritual things without which we cannot win through.

I repeat that the United States can accept no result save victory, final and complete. Not only must the shame of Japanese treachery be wiped out, but the sources of international brutality, wherever they exist, must be absolutely and finally broken.

In my message to the Congress yesterday I said that we "will make very certain that this form of treachery shall never again endanger us." In order to achieve that certainty, we must begin the great task that is before us by abandoning once and for all the illusion that we can ever again isolate ourselves from the rest of humanity.

In these past few years—and, most violently, in the past three days—we have learned a terrible lesson.

It is our obligation to our dead—it is our sacred obligation to their children and to our children—that we must never forget what we have learned.

And what we have learned is this:

There is no such thing as security for any nation—or any individual—in a world ruled by the principles of gangsterism.

There is no such thing as impregnable defense against powerful aggressors who sneak up in the dark and strike without warning.

We have learned that our ocean-girt hemisphere is not immune from severe attack—that we cannot measure our safety in terms of miles on any map any more.

We may acknowledge that our enemies have performed a brilliant feat of deception, perfectly timed and executed with great skill. It was a thoroughly dishonorable deed, but we must face the fact that modern warfare as conducted in the Nazi manner is a dirty business. We don't like it—we didn't want to get in it—but we are in it and we're going to fight it with everything we've got.

I do not think any American has any doubt of our ability to administer proper punishment to the perpetrators of these crimes.

Your government knows that for weeks Germany has been telling Japan that if Japan did not attack the United States, Japan would not share in dividing the spoils with Germany when peace came. She was promised by Germany that if she came in she would receive the complete and perpetual control of the whole of the Pacific area—and that means not only the Ear East, but also all of the Islands in the Pacific, and also a stranglehold on the west coast of North, Central and South America.

We know also that Germany and Japan are conducting their military and naval operations in accordance with a joint plan. That plan considers all peoples and nations which are not helping the Axis powers as common enemies of each and every one of the Axis powers.

That is their simple and obvious grand strategy. And that is why the American people must realize that it can be matched only with similar grand strategy. We must realize for example that Japanese successes against the United States in the Pacific are helpful to German operations in Libya; that any German success against the Caucasus is inevitably an assistance to Japan in her operations against the Dutch East Indies; that a German attack against Algiers or Morocco opens the way to a German attack against South America and the Canal.

On the other side of the picture, we must learn also to know that guerrilla warfare against the Germans in, let us say Serbia or Norway, helps us; that a successful Russian offensive against the Germans helps us; and that British successes on land or sea in any part of the world strengthen our hands.

Remember always that Germany and Italy, regardless of any formal declaration of war, consider themselves at war with the United States at this moment just as much as they consider themselves at war with Britain or Russia. And Germany puts all the other Republics of the Americas into the same category of enemies. The people of our sister Republics of this Hemisphere can be honored by that fact.

The true goal we seek is far above and beyond the ugly field of battle. When we resort to force, as now we must, we are determined that this force shall be directed toward ultimate good as well as against immediate evil. We Americans are not destroyers—we are builders.

We are now in the midst of a war, not for conquest, not for vengeance, but for a world in which this nation, and all that this nation represents, will be safe for our children. We expect to eliminate the danger from Japan, but it would serve us ill if we accomplished that and found that the rest of the world was dominated by Hitler and Mussolini.

So we are going to win the war and we are going to win the peace that follows.

And in the difficult hours of this day—through dark days that may be yet to come—we will know that the vast majority of the members of the human race are on our side. Many of them are fighting with us. All of them are praying for us. But, in representing our cause, we represent theirs as well—our hope and their hope for liberty under God.

February 23, 1942.

My Fellow Americans:

Washington's Birthday is a most appropriate occasion for us to talk with each other about things as they are today and things as we know they shall be in the future.

For eight years, General Washington and his Continental Army were faced continually with formidable odds and recurring defeats. Supplies and equipment were lacking. In a sense, every winter was a Valley Forge. Throughout the thirteen states there existed fifth columnists—and selfish men, jealous men, fearful men, who proclaimed that Washington's cause was hopeless, and that he should ask for a negotiated peace.

Washington's conduct in those hard times has provided the model for all Americans ever since—a model of moral stamina. He held to his course, as it had been charted in the Declaration of Independence. He and the brave men who served with him knew that no man's life or fortune was secure without freedom and free institutions.

The present great struggle has taught us increasingly that freedom of person and security of property anywhere in the world depend upon the security of the rights and obligations of liberty and justice everywhere in the world.

This war is a new kind of war. It is different from all other wars of the past, not only in its methods and weapons but also in its geography. It is warfare in terms of every continent, every island, every sea, every air lane in the world.

That is the reason why I have asked you to take out and spread before you a map of the whole earth, and to follow with me in the references which I shall make to the world-encircling battle lines of this war. Many questions will, I fear, remain unanswered tonight; but I know you will realize that I cannot cover everything in any one short report to the people.

The broad oceans which have been heralded in the past as our protection from attack have become endless battlefields on which we are constantly being challenged by our enemies.

We must all understand and face the hard fact that our job now is to fight at distances which extend all the way around the globe.

We fight at these vast distances because that is where our enemies are. Until our flow of supplies gives us clear superiority we must keep on striking our enemies wherever and whenever we can meet them, even if, for a while, we have to yield ground. Actually, though, we are taking a heavy toll of the enemy every day that goes by.

We must fight at these vast distances to protect our supply lines and our lines of communication with our allies—protect these lines from the enemies who are bending every ounce of their strength, striving against time, to cut them. The object of the Nazis and the Japanese is to separate the United States, Britain, China and Russia, and to isolate them one from another, so that each will be surrounded and cut off from sources of supplies and reinforcements. It is the old familiar Axis policy of "divide and conquer."

There are those who still think, however, in terms of the days of sailing-ships. They advise us to pull our warships and our planes and our merchant ships into our own home waters and concentrate solely on last ditch defense. But let me illustrate what would happen if we followed such foolish advice.

Look at your map. Look at the vast area of China, with its millions of fighting men. Look at the vast area of Russia, with its powerful armies and proven military might. Look at the British Isles, Australia, New Zealand, the Dutch Indies, India, the Near East and the Continent of Africa, with their resources of raw materials, and of peoples determined to resist Axis domination. Look too at North America, Central America and South America.

It is obvious what would happen if all of these great reservoirs of power were cut off from each other either by enemy action or by self-imposed isolation:

First, in such a case, we could no longer send aid of any kind to China—to the brave people who, for nearly five years, have withstood Japanese assault, destroyed hundreds of thousands of Japanese soldiers and vast quantities of Japanese war munitions. It is essential that we help China in her magnificent defense and in her inevitable counteroffensive—for that is one important element in the ultimate defeat of Japan.

Second, if we lost communication with the southwest Pacific, all of that area, including Australia and New Zealand and the Dutch Indies, would fall under Japanese domination. Japan in such a case could release great numbers of ships and men to launch attacks on a large scale against the coasts of the Western Hemisphere—South America and Central America, and North America—including Alaska. At the same time, she could immediately extend her conquests in the other direction toward India, and through the Indian Ocean to Africa, to the Near East, and try to join forces with Germany and Italy.

Third, if we were to stop sending munitions to the British and the Russians in the Mediterranean, in the Persian Gulf and the Red Sea, we would be helping the Nazis to overrun Turkey, Syria, Iraq, Persia, Egypt and the Suez Canal, the whole coast of North Africa itself, and with that inevitably the whole coast of West Africa—putting Germany within easy striking distance of South America—fifteen hundred miles away.

Fourth, if by such a fatuous policy we ceased to protect the North Atlantic
   supply line to Britain and to Russia, we would help to cripple the splendid
   counter-offensive by Russia against the Nazis, and we would help to deprive
   Britain of essential food supplies and munitions.

Those Americans who believed that we could live under the illusion of isolationism wanted the American eagle to imitate the tactics of the ostrich. Now, many of those same people, afraid that we may be sticking our necks out, want our national bird to be turned into a turtle. But we prefer to retain the eagle as it is—flying high and striking hard.

I know that I speak for the mass of the American people when I say that we reject the turtle policy and will continue increasingly the policy of carrying the war to the enemy in distant lands and distant waters—as far away as possible from our own home grounds.

There are four main lines of communication now being travelled by our ships: the North Atlantic, the South Atlantic, the Indian Ocean and the South Pacific. These routes are not one-way streets, for the ships that carry our troops and munitions outbound bring back essential raw materials which we require for our own use.

The maintenance of these vital lines is a very tough job. It is a job which requires tremendous daring, tremendous resourcefulness, and, above all, tremendous production of planes and tanks and guns and also of the ships to carry them. And I speak again for the American people when I say that we can and will do that job.

The defense of the world-wide lines of communication demands relatively safe use by us of the sea and of the air along the various routes; and this, in turn, depends upon control by the United Nations of many strategic bases along those routes.

Control of the air involves the simultaneous use of two types of planes—first, the long-range heavy bomber; and, second, the light bombers, dive bombers, torpedo planes, and short-range pursuit planes, all of which are essential to the protection of the bases and of the bombers themselves.

Heavy bombers can fly under their own power from here to the southwest Pacific, but the smaller planes cannot. Therefore, these lighter planes have to be packed in crates and sent on board cargo ships. Look at your map again; and you will see that the route is long—and at many places perilous—either across the South Atlantic all the way around South Africa and the Cape of Good Hope, or from California to the East Indies direct. A vessel can make a round trip by either route in about four months, or only three round trips in a whole year.

In spite of the length, and in spite of the difficulties of this transportation, I can tell you that in two and a half months we already have a large number of bombers and pursuit planes, manned by American pilots and crews, which are now in daily contact with the enemy in the Southwest Pacific. And thousands of American troops are today in that area engaged in operations not only in the air but on the ground as well.

In this battle area, Japan has had an obvious initial advantage. For she could fly even her short-range planes to the points of attack by using many stepping stones open to her—bases in a multitude of Pacific islands and also bases on the China coast, Indo-China coast, and in Thailand and Malaya coasts. Japanese troop transports could go south from Japan and from China through the narrow China Sea, which can be protected by Japanese planes throughout its whole length.

I ask you to look at your maps again, particularly at that portion of the Pacific Ocean lying west of Hawaii. Before this war even started, the Philippine Islands were already surrounded on three sides by Japanese power. On the west, the China side, the Japanese were in possession of the coast of China and the coast of Indo-China which had been yielded to them by the Vichy French. On the North are the islands of Japan themselves, reaching down almost to northern Luzon. On the east are the Mandated Islands—which Japan had occupied exclusively, and had fortified in absolute violation of her written word.

The islands that lie between Hawaii and the Philippines—these islands, hundreds of them, appear only as small dots on most maps. But they cover a large strategic area. Guam lies in the middle of them—a lone outpost which we have never fortified.

Under the Washington Treaty of 1921 we had solemnly agreed not to add to the fortification of the Philippines. We had no safe naval bases there, so we could not use the islands for extensive naval operations.

Immediately after this war started, the Japanese forces moved down on either side of the Philippines to numerous points south of them—thereby completely encircling the Philippines from north, south, east and west.

It is that complete encirclement, with control of the air by Japanese land-based aircraft, which has prevented us from sending substantial reinforcements of men and material to the gallant defenders of the Philippines. For forty years it has always been our strategy—a strategy born of necessity—that in the event of a full-scale attack on the Islands by Japan, we should fight a delaying action, attempting to retire slowly into Bataan Peninsula and Corregidor.

We knew that the war as a whole would have to be fought and won by a process of attrition against Japan itself. We knew all along that, with our greater resources, we could ultimately out-build Japan and ultimately overwhelm her on sea, and on land and in the air. We knew that, to obtain our objective, many varieties of operations would be necessary in areas other than the Philippines.

Now nothing that has occurred in the past two months has caused us to revise this basic strategy of necessity—except that the defense put up by General MacArthur has magnificently exceeded the previous estimates of endurance, and he and his men are gaining eternal glory therefore.

MacArthur's army of Filipinos and Americans, and the forces of the United Nations in China, in Burma and the Netherlands East Indies, are all together fulfilling the same essential task. They are making Japan pay an increasingly terrible price for her ambitious attempts to seize control of the whole Asiatic world. Every Japanese transport sunk off Java is one less transport that they can use to carry reinforcements to their army opposing General MacArthur in Luzon.

It has been said that Japanese gains in the Philippines were made possible only by the success of their surprise attack on Pearl Harbor. I tell you that this is not so.

Even if the attack had not been made your map will show that it would have been a hopeless operation for us to send the Fleet to the Philippines through thousands of miles of ocean, while all those island bases were under the sole control of the Japanese.

The consequences of the attack on Pearl Harbor—serious as they were—have been wildly exaggerated in other ways. And these exaggerations come originally from Axis propagandists; but they have been repeated, I regret to say, by Americans in and out of public life.

You and I have the utmost contempt for Americans who, since Pearl Harbor, have whispered or announced "off the record" that there was no longer any

Pacific Fleet—that the Fleet was all sunk or destroyed on December 7th—that more than a thousand of our planes were destroyed on the ground. They have suggested slyly that the government has withheld the truth about casualties—that eleven or twelve thousand men were killed at Pearl Harbor instead of the figures as officially announced. They have even served the enemy propagandists by spreading the incredible story that ship-loads of bodies of our honored American dead were about to arrive in New York harbor to be put into a common grave.

Almost every Axis broadcast—Berlin, Rome, Tokyo—directly quotes Americans who, by speech or in the press, make damnable misstatements such as these.

The American people realize that in many cases details of military operations cannot be disclosed until we are absolutely certain that the announcement will not give to the enemy military information which he does not already possess.

Your government has unmistakable confidence in your ability to hear the worst, without flinching or losing heart. You must, in turn, have complete confidence that your government is keeping nothing from you except information that will help the enemy in his attempt to destroy us. In a democracy there is always a solemn pact of truth between government and the people, but there must also always be a full use of discretion, and that word "discretion" applies to the critics of government as well.

This is war. The American people want to know, and will be told, the general trend of how the war is going. But they do not wish to help the enemy any more than our fighting forces do, and they will pay little attention to the rumor-mongers and the poison peddlers in our midst.

To pass from the realm of rumor and poison to the field of facts: the number of our officers and men killed in the attack on Pearl Harbor on December seventh was 2,340, and the number wounded was 940. Of all of the combatant ships based on Pearl Harbor—battleships, heavy cruisers, light cruisers, aircraft carriers, destroyers and submarines—only three are permanently put out of commission.

Very many of the ships of the Pacific Fleet were not even in Pearl Harbor. Some of those that were there were hit very slightly, and others that were damaged have either rejoined the fleet by now or are still undergoing repairs.

And when those repairs are completed, the ships will be more efficient fighting machines than they were before.

The report that we lost more than a thousand planes at Pearl Harbor is as baseless as the other weird rumors. The Japanese do not know just how many planes they destroyed that day, and I am not going to tell them. But I can say that to date—and including Pearl Harbor—we have destroyed considerably more Japanese planes than they have destroyed of ours.

We have most certainly suffered losses—from Hitler's U-Boats in the Atlantic as well as from the Japanese in the Pacific—and we shall suffer more of them before the turn of the tide. But, speaking for the United States of America, let me say once and for all to the people of the world: We Americans have been compelled to yield ground, but we will regain it. We and the other United Nations are committed to the destruction of the militarism of Japan and Germany. We are daily increasing our strength. Soon, we and not our enemies, will have the offensive; we, not they, will win the final battles; and we, not they, will make the final peace.

Conquered nations in Europe know what the yoke of the Nazis is like. And the people of Korea and of Manchuria know in their flesh the harsh despotism of Japan. All of the people of Asia know that if there is to be an honorable and decent future for any of them or any of us, that future depends on victory by the United Nations over the forces of Axis enslavement.

If a just and durable peace is to be attained, or even if all of us are merely to save our own skins, there is one thought for us here at home to keep uppermost—the fulfillment of our special task of production.

Germany, Italy and Japan are very close to their maximum output of planes, guns, tanks and ships. The United Nations are not—especially the United States of America.

Our first job then is to build up production—uninterrupted production—so that the United Nations can maintain control of the seas and attain control of the air—not merely a slight superiority, but an overwhelming superiority.

On January 6th of this year, I set certain definite goals of production for airplanes, tanks, guns and ships. The Axis propagandists called them fantastic. Tonight, nearly two months later, and after a careful survey of progress by Donald Nelson and others charged with responsibility for our production, I can tell you that those goals will be attained.

In every part of the country, experts in production and the men and women at work in the plants are giving loyal service. With few exceptions, labor, capital and farming realize that this is no time either to make undue profits or to gain special advantages, one over the other.

We are calling for new plants and additions—additions to old plants. We are calling for plant conversion to war needs. We are seeking more men and more women to run them. We are working longer hours. We are coming to realize that one extra plane or extra tank or extra gun or extra ship completed tomorrow may, in a few months, turn the tide on some distant battlefield; it may make the difference between life and death for some of our own fighting men. We know now that if we lose this war it will be generations or even centuries before our conception of democracy can live again. And we can lose this war only if use slow up our effort or if we waste our ammunition sniping at each other.

Here are three high purposes for every American:

1. We shall not stop work for a single day. If any dispute arises we shall keep on working while the dispute is solved by mediation, or conciliation or arbitration—until the war is won.
2. We shall not demand special gains or special privileges or special advantages for any one group or occupation.
3. We shall give up conveniences and modify the routine of our lives if our country asks us to do so. We will do it cheerfully, remembering that the common enemy seeks to destroy every home and every freedom in every part of our land.

This generation of Americans has come to realize, with a present and personal realization, that there is something larger and more important than the life of any individual or of any individual group—something for which a man will sacrifice, and gladly sacrifice, not only his pleasures, not only his goods, not only his associations with those he loves, but his life itself. In time of crisis when the future is in the balance, we come to understand, with full recognition and devotion, what this nation is and what we owe to it.

The Axis propagandists have tried in various evil ways to destroy our determination and our morale. Failing in that, they are now trying to destroy our confidence in our own allies. They say that the British are finished—that the

Russians and the Chinese are about to quit. Patriotic and sensible Americans will reject these absurdities. And instead of listening to any of this crude propaganda, they will recall some of the things that Nazis and Japanese have said and are still saying about us.

Ever since this nation became the arsenal of democracy—ever since enactment of Lend-Lease—there has been one persistent theme through all Axis propaganda.

This theme has been that Americans are admittedly rich, that Americans have considerable industrial power—but that Americans are soft and decadent, that they cannot and will not unite and work and fight.

From Berlin, Rome and Tokyo we have been described as a nation of weaklings—"playboys"—who would hire British soldiers, or Russian soldiers, or Chinese soldiers to do our fighting for us.

Let them repeat that now!

Let them tell that to General MacArthur and his men.

Let them tell that to the sailors who today are hitting hard in the far waters of the Pacific.

Let them tell that to the boys in the Flying Fortresses.

Let them tell that to the Marines!

The United Nations constitute an association of independent peoples of equal dignity and equal importance. The United Nations are dedicated to a common cause. We share equally and with equal zeal the anguish and the awful sacrifices of war. In the partnership of our common enterprise, we must share in a unified plan in which all of us must play our several parts, each of us being equally indispensable and dependent one on the other.

We have unified command and cooperation and comradeship.

We Americans will contribute unified production and unified acceptance of sacrifice and of effort. That means a national unity that can know no limitations of race or creed or selfish politics. The American people expect that much from themselves. And the American people will find ways and means of expressing their determination to their enemies, including the Japanese Admiral who has said that he will dictate the terms of peace here in the White House.

We of the United Nations are agreed on certain broad principles in the kind of peace we seek. The Atlantic Charter applies not only to the parts of the world that border the Atlantic but to the whole world; disarmament of aggressors, self-determination of nations and peoples, and the four freedoms—freedom of speech, freedom of religion, freedom from want, and freedom from fear.

The British and the Russian people have known the full fury of Nazi onslaught. There have been times when the fate of London and Moscow was in serious doubt. But there was never the slightest question that either the British or the Russians would yield. And today all the United Nations salute the superb Russian Army as it celebrates the twenty-fourth anniversary of its first assembly.

Though their homeland was overrun, the Dutch people are still fighting stubbornly and powerfully overseas.

The great Chinese people have suffered grievous losses; Chungking has been almost wiped out of existence—yet it remains the capital of an unbeatable China.

That is the conquering spirit which prevails throughout the United Nations in this war.

The task that we Americans now face will test us to the uttermost. Never before have we been called upon for such a prodigious effort. Never before have we had so little time in which to do so much.

"These are the times that try men's souls." Tom Paine wrote those words on a drumhead, by the light of a campfire. That was when Washington's little army of ragged, rugged men was retreating across New Jersey, having tasted nothing but defeat.

And General Washington ordered that these great words written by Tom Paine be read to the men of every regiment in the Continental Army, and this was the assurance given to the first American armed forces:

"The summer soldier and the sunshine patriot will, in this crisis, shrink from the service of their country; but he that stands it now, deserves the love and thanks of man and woman. Tyranny, like hell, is not easily conquered, yet we have this consolation with us, that the harder the sacrifice, the more glorious the triumph."

So spoke Americans in the year 1776.

So speak Americans today!

April 28, 1942.

My Fellow Americans:

It is nearly five months since we were attacked at Pearl Harbor. For the two years prior to that attack this country had been gearing itself up to a high level of production of munitions. And yet our war efforts had done little to dislocate the normal lives of most of us.

Since then we have dispatched strong forces of our Army and Navy, several hundred thousand of them, to bases and battlefronts thousands of miles from home. We have stepped up our war production on a scale that is testing our industrial power, our engineering genius and our economic structure to the utmost. We have had no illusions about the fact that this is a tough job—and a long one.

American warships are now in combat in the North and South Atlantic, in the Arctic, in the Mediterranean, in the Indian Ocean, and in the North and South Pacific. American troops have taken stations in South America, Greenland, Iceland, the British Isles, the Near East, the Middle East and the Far East, the continent of Australia, and many islands of the Pacific. American war planes, manned by Americans, are flying in actual combat over all the continents and all the oceans.

On the European front the most important development of the past year has been without question the crushing counteroffensive on the part of the great armies of Russia against the powerful German army. These Russian forces have destroyed and are destroying more armed power of our enemies—troops, planes, tanks and guns—than all the other United Nations put together.

In the Mediterranean area, matters remain on the surface much as they were. But the situation there is receiving very careful attention.

Recently we received news of a change in government in what we used to know as the Republic of France—a name dear to the hearts of all lovers of liberty—a name and an institution which we hope will soon be restored to full dignity.

Throughout the Nazi occupation of France, we have hoped for the maintenance of a French government which would strive to regain independence, to reestablish the principles of "Liberty, Equality and Fraternity," and to restore the historic culture of France. Our policy has been consistent from the very beginning. However, we are now greatly concerned lest those who have recently come to power may seek to force the brave French people into submission to Nazi despotism.

The United Nations will take measures, if necessary, to prevent the use of French territory in any part of the world for military purposes by the Axis powers. The good people of France will readily understand that such action is essential for the United Nations to prevent assistance to the armies or navies or air forces of Germany, or Italy or Japan. The overwhelming majority of the French people understand that the fight of the United Nations is fundamentally their fight, that our victory means the restoration of a free and independent France—and the saving of France from the slavery which would be imposed upon her by her external enemies and by her internal traitors.

We know how the French people really feel. We know that a deep- seated determination to obstruct every step in the Axis plan extends from occupied France through Vichy France all the way to the people of their colonies in every ocean and on every continent.

Our planes are helping in the defense of French colonies today, and soon American Flying Fortresses will be fighting for the liberation of the darkened continent of Europe itself.

In all the occupied countries there are men and women, and even little children who have never stopped fighting, never stopped resisting, never stopped proving to the Nazis that their so-called "New Order" will never be enforced upon free peoples.

In the German and Italian peoples themselves there is a growing conviction that the cause of Nazism and Fascism is hopeless—that their political and military leaders have led them along the bitter road which leads not to world conquest but to final defeat. They cannot fail to contrast the present frantic speeches of these leaders with their arrogant boastings of a year ago, and two years ago.

On the other side of the world, in the Far East, we have passed through a phase of serious losses.

We have inevitably lost control of a large portion of the Philippine Islands. But this whole nation pays tribute to the Filipino and American officers and men who held out so long on Bataan Peninsula, to those grim and gallant fighters who still hold Corregidor, where the flag flies, and to the forces that are still striking effectively at the enemy on Mindanao and other islands.

The Malayan Peninsula and Singapore are in the hands of the enemy; the Netherlands East Indies are almost entirely occupied, though resistance there continues. Many other islands are in the possession of the Japanese. But there is good reason to believe that their southward advance has been checked. Australia, New Zealand, and much other territory will be bases for offensive action—and we are determined that the territory that has been lost will be regained.

The Japanese are pressing their northward advance against Burma with considerable power, driving toward India and China. They have been opposed with great bravery by small British and Chinese forces aided by American fliers.

The news in Burma tonight is not good. The Japanese may cut the Burma Road; but I want to say to the gallant people of China that no matter what advances the Japanese may make, ways will be found to deliver airplanes and munitions of war to the armies of Generalissimo Chiang Kai-shek.

We remember that the Chinese people were the first to stand up and fight against the aggressors in this war; and in the future a still unconquerable China will play its proper role in maintaining peace and prosperity, not only in Eastern Asia but in the whole world.

For every advance that the Japanese have made since they started their frenzied career of conquest, they have had to pay a very heavy toll in warships, in transports, in planes, and in men. They are feeling the effects of those losses.

It is even reported from Japan that somebody has dropped bombs on Tokyo, and on other principal centers of Japanese war industries. If this be true, it is the first time in history that Japan has suffered such indignities.

Although the treacherous attack on Pearl Harbor was the immediate cause of our entry into the war, that event found the American people spiritually prepared for war on a world-wide scale. We went into this war fighting. We know what we are fighting for. We realize that the war has become what Hitler originally proclaimed it to be—a total war.

Not all of us can have the privilege of fighting our enemies in distant parts of the world.

Not all of us can have the privilege of working in a munitions factory or a shipyard, or on the farms or in oil fields or mines, producing the weapons or the raw materials that are needed by our armed forces.

But there is one front and one battle where everyone in the United States—every man, woman, and child—is in action, and will be privileged to remain in action throughout this war. That front is right here at home, in our daily lives, and in our daily tasks. Here at home everyone will have the privilege of making whatever self-denial is necessary, not only to supply our fighting men, but to keep the economic structure of our country fortified and secure during the war and after the war. This will require, of course, the abandonment not only of luxuries but of many other creature comforts.

Every loyal American is aware of his individual responsibility. Whenever I hear anyone saying "The American people are complacent—they need to be aroused," I feel like asking him to come to Washington to read the mail that floods into the White House and into all departments of this government. The one question that recurs through all these thousands of letters and messages is "What more can I do to help my country in winning this war"?

To build the factories, to buy the materials, to pay the labor, to provide the transportation, to equip and feed and house the soldiers, sailors and marines, and to do all the thousands of things necessary in a war—all cost a lot of money, more money than has ever been spent by any nation at any time in the long history of the world.

We are now spending, solely for war purposes, the sum of about one hundred million dollars every day in the week. But, before this year is over, that almost unbelievable rate of expenditure will be doubled.

All of this money has to be spent—and spent quickly—if we are to produce within the time now available the enormous quantities of weapons of war which we need. But the spending of these tremendous sums presents grave danger of disaster to our national economy.

When your government continues to spend these unprecedented sums for munitions month by month and year by year, that money goes into the pocketbooks and bank accounts of the people of the United States. At the same time raw materials and many manufactured goods are necessarily taken away from civilian use, and machinery and factories are being converted to war production.

You do not have to be a professor of mathematics or economics to see that if people with plenty of cash start bidding against each other for scarce goods, the price of those goods goes up.

Yesterday I submitted to the Congress of the United states a seven- point program of general principles which taken together could be called the national economic policy for attaining the great objective of keeping the cost of living down.

I repeat them now to you in substance:

First. we must, through heavier taxes, keep personal and corporate profits at a low reasonable rate.

Second. We must fix ceilings on prices and rents.

Third. We must stabilize wages.

Fourth. We must stabilize farm prices.

Fifth. We must put more billions into war bonds.

Sixth. We must ration all essential commodities which are scarce.

Seventh. We must discourage installment buying, and encourage paying off debts and mortgages.

I do not think it is necessary to repeat what I said yesterday to the Congress in discussing these general principles.

The important thing to remember is that each one of these points is dependent on the others if the whole program is to work.

Some people are already taking the position that every one of the seven points is correct except the one point which steps on their own individual toes. A few seem very willing to approve self- denial—on the part of their neighbors. The only effective course of action is a simultaneous attack on all of the factors which increase the cost of living, in one comprehensive, all-embracing program covering prices, and profits, and wages, and taxes and debts.

The blunt fact is that every single person in the United States is going to be affected by this program. Some of you will be affected more directly by one or two of these restrictive measures, but all of you will be affected indirectly by all of them.

Are you a businessman, or do you own stock in a business corporation? Well, your profits are going to be cut down to a reasonably low level by taxation.

Your income will be subject to higher taxes. Indeed in these days, when every available dollar should go to the war effort, I do not think that any American citizen should have a net income in excess of $25,000 per year after payment of taxes.

Are you a retailer or a wholesaler or a manufacturer or a farmer or a landlord? Ceilings are being placed on the prices at which you can sell your goods or rent your property.

Do you work for wages? You will have to forego higher wages for your particular job for the duration of the war.

All of us are used to spending money for things that we want, things, however, which are not absolutely essential. We will all have to forego that kind of spending. Because we must put every dime and every dollar we can possibly spare out of our earnings into war bonds and stamps. Because the demands of the war effort require the rationing of goods of which there is not enough to go around. Because the stopping of purchases of non-essentials will release thousands of workers who are needed in the war effort.

As I told the Congress yesterday, "sacrifice" is not exactly the proper word with which to describe this program of self-denial. When, at the end of this great struggle we shall have saved our free way of life, we shall have made no "sacrifice."

The price for civilization must be paid in hard work and sorrow and blood. The price is not too high. If you doubt it, ask those millions who live today under the tyranny of Hitlerism.

Ask the workers of France and Norway and the Netherlands, whipped to labor by the lash, whether the stabilization of wages is too great a "sacrifice."

Ask the farmers of Poland and Denmark, of Czechoslovakia and France, looted of their livestock, starving while their own crops are stolen from their land, ask them whether "parity" prices are too great a "sacrifice."

Ask the businessmen of Europe, whose enterprises have been stolen from their owners, whether the limitation of profits and personal incomes is too great a "sacrifice."

Ask the women and children whom Hitler is starving whether the rationing of tires and gasoline and sugar is too great a "sacrifice."

We do not have to ask them. They have already given us their agonized answers.

This great war effort must be carried through to its victorious conclusion by the indomitable will and determination of the people as one great whole.

It must not be impeded by the faint of heart.

It must not be impeded by those who put their own selfish interests above the interests of the nation.

It must not be impeded by those who pervert honest criticism into falsification of fact.

It must not be impeded by self-styled experts either in economics or military problems who know neither true figures nor geography itself.

It must not be impeded by a few bogus patriots who use the sacred freedom of the press to echo the sentiments of the propagandists in Tokyo and Berlin.

And, above all, it shall not be imperiled by the handful of noisy traitors—betrayers of America, betrayers of Christianity itself—would-be dictators who in their hearts and souls have yielded to Hitlerism and would have this Republic do likewise.

I shall use all of the executive power that I have to carry out the policy laid down. If it becomes necessary to ask for any additional legislation in order to attain our objective of preventing a spiral in the cost of living, I shall do so.

I know the American farmer, the American workman, and the American businessman. I know that they will gladly embrace this economy and equality of sacrifice, satisfied that it is necessary for the most vital and compelling motive in all their lives—winning through to victory.

Never in the memory of man has there been a war in which the courage, the endurance and the loyalty of civilians played so vital a part.

Many thousands of civilians all over the world have been and are being killed or maimed by enemy action. Indeed, it was the fortitude of the common people of Britain under fire which enabled that island to stand and prevented Hitler from winning the war in 1940. The ruins of London and Coventry and other cities are today the proudest monuments to British heroism.

Our own American civilian population is now relatively safe from such disasters. And, to an ever-increasing extent, our soldiers, sailors and marines are fighting with great bravery and great skill on far distant fronts to make sure that we shall remain safe.

I should like to tell you one or two stories about the men we have in our armed forces:

There is, for example, Dr. Corydon M. Wassell. He was a missionary, well known for his good works in China. He is a simple, modest, retiring man, nearly sixty years old, but he entered the service of his country and was commissioned a Lieutenant Commander in the Navy.

Dr. Wassell was assigned to duty in Java caring for wounded officers and men of the cruisers HOUSTON and MARBLEHEAD which had been in heavy action in the Java seas.

When the Japanese advanced across the island, it was decided to evacuate as many as possible of the wounded to Australia. But about twelve of the men were so badly wounded that they could not be moved. Dr. Wassell remained with these men, knowing that he would be captured by the enemy. But he decided to make a last desperate attempt to get the men out of Java. He asked each of them if he wished to take the chance, and every one agreed.

He first had to get the twelve men to the sea coast—fifty miles away. To do this, he had to improvise stretchers for the hazardous journey. The men were suffering severely, but Dr. Wassell kept them alive by his skill, and inspired them by his own courage.

And as the official report said, Dr. Wassell was "almost like a Christ-like shepherd devoted to his flock."

On the sea coast, he embarked the men on a little Dutch ship. They were bombed, they were machine-gunned by waves of Japanese planes. Dr. Wassell took virtual command of the ship, and by great skill avoided destruction, hiding in little bays and little inlets.

A few days later, Dr. Wassell and his small flock of wounded men reached Australia safely.

And today Dr. Wassell wears the Navy Cross.

Another story concerns a ship, a ship rather than an individual man.

You may remember the tragic sinking of the submarine, the U.S.S. SQUALUS off the New England coast in the summer of 1939. Some of the crew were lost, but others were saved by the speed and the efficiency of the surface rescue crews. The SQUALUS itself was tediously raised from the bottom of the sea.

She was repaired and put back into commission, and eventually she sailed again under a new name, the U.S.S. SAILFISH. Today, she is a potent and effective unit of our submarine fleet in the Southwest Pacific.

The SAILFISH has covered many thousands of miles in operations in those waters.

She has sunk a Japanese destroyer.

She has torpedoed a Japanese cruiser.

She has made torpedo hits—two of them—on a Japanese aircraft carrier.

Three of the enlisted men of our Navy who went down with the SQUALUS in 1939 and were rescued, are today serving on the same ship, the U.S.S. SAILFISH, in this war.

It seems to me that it is heartening to know that the SQUALUS, once given up as lost, rose from the depths to fight for our country in time of peril.

One more story, that I heard only this morning:

This is a story of one of our Army Flying Fortresses operating in the Western Pacific. The pilot of this plane is a modest young man, proud of his crew for one of the toughest fights a bomber has yet experienced.

The bomber departed from its base, as part or a flight of five bombers, to attack Japanese transports that were landing troops against us in the Philippines. When they had gone about halfway to their destination, one of the motors of this bomber went out of commission. The young pilot lost contact with the other bombers. The crew, however, got the motor working, got it going again and the plane proceeded on its mission alone.

By the time it arrived at its target the other four Flying Fortresses had already passed over, had dropped their bombs, and had stirred up the hornets' nest of Japanese "Zero" planes. Eighteen of these "Zero" fighters attacked our one Flying Fortress. Despite this mass attack, our plane proceeded on its mission, and dropped all of its bombs on six Japanese transports which were lined up along the docks.

As it turned back on its homeward journey a running fight between the bomber and the eighteen Japanese pursuit planes continued for 75 miles. Four pursuit planes of the Japs attacked simultaneously at each side. Four were shot down with the side guns. During this fight, the bomber's radio operator was killed, the engineer's right hand was shot off, and one gunner was crippled, leaving only one man available to operate both side guns. Although wounded in one hand, this gunner alternately manned both side guns, bringing down three more Japanese "Zero" planes. While this was going on, one engine on the American bomber was shot out, one gas tank was hit, the radio was shot off, and the oxygen system was entirely destroyed. Out of eleven control cables all but four were shot away. The rear landing wheel was blown off entirely, and the two front wheels were both shot flat.

The fight continued until the remaining Japanese pursuit ships exhausted their ammunition and turned back. With two engines gone and the plane practically out of control, the American bomber returned to its base after dark and made an emergency landing. The mission had been accomplished.

The name of that pilot is Captain Hewitt T. Wheless, of the United States Army. He comes from a place called Menard, Texas—with a population 2,375. He has been awarded the Distinguished Service Cross. And I hope that he is listening.

These stories I have told you are not exceptional. They are typical examples of individual heroism and skill.

As we here at home contemplate our own duties, our own responsibilities, let us think and think hard of the example which is being set for us by our fighting men.

Our soldiers and sailors are members of well disciplined units. But they are still and forever individuals—free individuals. They are farmers, and workers, businessmen, professional men, artists, clerks.

They are the United States of America.

That is why they fight.

We too are the United States of America.

That is why we must work and sacrifice.

It is for them. It is for us. It is for victory.

September 7, 1942.

My Friends:

I wish that all the Americans people could read all the citations for various medals recommended for our soldiers and sailors and marines. I am picking out one of these citations which tells of the accomplishments of Lieutenant John James Powers, United States Navy, during three days of the battles with Japanese forces in the Coral Sea.

During the first two days, Lieutenant Powers, flying a dive-bomber in the face of blasting enemy anti-aircraft fire, demolished one large enemy gunboat, put another gunboat out of commission, severely damaged an aircraft tender and a twenty-thousand-ton transport, and scored a direct hit on an aircraft carrier which burst into flames and sank soon after.

The official citation then describes the morning of the third day of battle. As the pilots of his squadron left the ready room to man their planes, Lieutenant Powers said to them, "Remember, the folks back home are counting on us. I am going to get a hit if I have to lay it on their flight deck.

He led his section down to the target from an altitude of 18,000 feet, through a wall of bursting anti-aircraft shells and swarms of enemy planes. He dived almost to the very deck of the enemy carrier, and did not release his bomb until he was sure of a direct hit. He was last seen attempting recovery from his dive at the extremely low altitude of two hundred feet, amid a terrific barrage of shell and bomb fragments, and smoke and flame and debris from the stricken vessel. His own plane was destroyed by the explosion of his own bomb. But he had made good his promise to "lay it on their flight deck."

I have received a recommendation from the Secretary of the Navy that Lieutenant John James Powers of New York City, missing in action, be awarded the Medal of Honor. I hereby and now make this award.

You and I are "the folks back home" for whose protection Lieutenant Powers fought and repeatedly risked his life. He said that we counted on him and his men. We did not count in vain. But have not those men a right to be counting on us? How are we playing our part "back home" in winning this war?

The answer is that we are not doing enough.

Today I sent a message to the Congress, pointing out the overwhelming urgency of the serious domestic economic crisis with which we are threatened. Some call it "inflation," which is a vague sort of term, and others call it a "rise in the cost of living," which is much more easily understood by most families.

That phrase, "the cost of living," means essentially what a dollar can buy.

From January 1, 1941, to May of this year, nearly a year and a half, the cost of living went up about 15 percent. And at that point last May we undertook to freeze the cost of living. But we could not do a complete job of it, because the Congressional authority at the time exempted a large part of farm products

146

used for food and for making clothing, although several weeks before, I had asked the Congress for legislation to stabilize all farm prices.

At that time I had told the Congress that there were seven elements in our national economy, all of which had to be controlled; and that if any one essential element remained exempt, the cost of living could not be held down.

On only two of these points—both of them vital however—did I call for Congressional action. These two vital points were: First, taxation; and, second, the stabilization of all farm prices at parity.

"Parity" is a standard for the maintenance of good farm prices. It was established as our national policy way back in 1933. It means that the farmer and the city worker are on the same relative ratio with each other in purchasing power as they were during a period some thirty years before—at a time then the farmer had a satisfactory purchasing power. One hundred percent of parity, therefore, has been accepted by farmers as the fair standard for the prices they receive.

Last January, however, the Congress passed a law forbidding ceilings on farm prices below 110 percent of parity on some commodities. And on other commodities the ceiling was even higher, so that the average possible ceiling is now about 116 percent of parity for agricultural products as a whole.

This act of favoritism for one particular group in the community increased the cost of food to everybody—not only to the workers in the city or in the munitions plants, and their families, but also to the families of the farmers themselves.

Since last May, ceilings have been set on nearly all commodities, rents services, except the exempted farm products. Installment buying, for example, has been effectively controlled.

Wages in certain key industries have been stabilized on the basis of the present cost of living.

But it is obvious to all of us that if the cost of food continues to go up, as it is doing at present, the wage earner, particularly in the lower brackets, will have a right to an increase in his wages. I think that would be essential justice and a practical necessity.

Our experience with the control of other prices during the past few months has brought out one important fact—the rising cost of living can be controlled, providing that all elements making up the cost of living are controlled at the same time. I think that also is an essential justice and a practical necessity. We know that parity prices for farm products not now controlled will not put up the cost of living more than a very small amount; but we also know that if we must go up to an average of 116 percent of parity for food and other farm products—which is necessary at present under the Emergency Price Control Act before we can control all farm prices—the cost of living will get well out of hand. We are face to face with this danger today. Let us meet it and remove it.

I realize that it may seem out of proportion to you to be over- stressing these economic problems at a time like this, when we are all deeply concerned about the news from far distant fields of battle. But I give you the solemn assurance that failure to solve this problem here at home—and to solve it now—will make more difficult the winning of this war.

If the vicious spiral of inflation ever gets under way, the whole economic system will stagger. Prices and wages will go up so rapidly that the entire production program will be endangered. The cost of the war, paid by taxpayers, will jump beyond all present calculations. It will mean an uncontrollable rise in prices and in wages, which can result in raising the overall cost of living as high as another 20 percent soon. That would mean that the purchasing power of every dollar that you have in your pay envelope, or in the bank, or included in your insurance policy or your pension, would be reduced to about eighty cents[1] worth. I need not tell you that this would have a demoralizing effect on our people, soldiers and civilians alike.

Overall stabilization of prices, and salaries, wages and profits is necessary to the continued increasing production of planes and tanks and ships and guns.

In my message to Congress today, I have said that this must be done quickly. If we wait for two or three or four or six months it may well be too late.

I have told the Congress that the administration cannot hold the actual cost of food and clothing down to the present level beyond October first.

Therefore, I have asked the Congress to pass legislation under which the President would be specifically authorized to stabilize the cost of living, including the price of all farm commodities. The purpose should be to hold farm prices at parity, or at levels of a recent date, whichever is higher. The purpose should also be to keep wages at a point stabilized with today's cost of living. Both must be regulated at the same time; and neither one of them can or should be regulated without the other.

At the same time that farm prices are stabilized, I will stabilize wages.

That is plain justice—and plain common sense.

And so I have asked the Congress to take this action by the first of October. We must now act with the dispatch which the stern necessities of war require.

I have told the Congress that inaction on their part by that date will leave me with an inescapable responsibility, a responsibility to the people of this country to see to it that the war effort is no longer imperiled by the threat of economic chaos.

As I said in my message to the Congress:

In the event that the Congress should fail to act, and act adequately, I shall accept the responsibility, and I will act.

The President has the powers, under the Constitution and under Congressional Acts, to take measures necessary to avert a disaster which would interfere with the winning of the war.

I have given the most careful and thoughtful consideration to meeting this issue without further reference to the Congress. I have determined, however, on this vital matter to consult with the Congress.

There may be those who will say that, if the situation is as grave as I have stated it to be, I should use my powers and act now. I can only say that I have approached this problem from every angle, and that I have decided that the course of conduct which I am following in this case is consistent with my sense of responsibility as President in time of war, and with my deep and unalterable devotion to the processes of democracy.

The responsibilities of the President in wartime to protect the nation are very grave. This total war, with our fighting fronts all over the world, makes the use of the executive power far more essential than in any previous war.

If we were invaded, the people of this country would expect the President to use any and all means to repel the invader.

Now the revolution and the war between the states were fought on our own soil, but today this war will be won or lost on other continents and in remote seas. I cannot tell what powers may have to be exercised in order to win this war.

The American people can be sure that I will use my powers with a full sense of responsibility to the Constitution and to my country. The American people can also be sure that I shall not hesitate to use every power vested in me to accomplish the defeat of our enemies in any part of the world where our own safety demands such defeat.

And when the war is over, the powers under which I act will automatically revert to the people of the United States—to the people to whom those powers belong.

I think I know the American farmers. I know they are as wholehearted in their patriotism as any other group. They have suffered from the constant fluctuations of farm prices—occasionally too high, more often too low. Nobody knows better than farmers the disastrous effects of wartime inflationary booms, and postwar deflationary panics.

So I have also suggested today that the Congress make our agricultural economy more stable. I have recommended that in addition to putting ceilings on all farm products now, we also place a definite floor under those prices for a period beginning now, continuing through the war, and for as long as necessary after the war. In this way we will be able to avoid the collapse of farm prices that happened after the last war. The farmers must be assured of a fair minimum price during the readjustment period which will follow the great, excessive world food demands which now prevail.

We must have some floor under farm prices, as we must have under wages, if we are to avoid the dangers of a postwar inflation on the one hand, or the catastrophe of a crash in farm prices and wages on the other.

Today I have also advised the Congress of the importance of speeding up the passage of the tax bill. The federal treasury is losing millions of dollars each and every day because the bill has not yet been passed. Taxation is the only practical way of preventing the incomes and profits of individuals and corporations from getting too high.

I have told the Congress once more that all net individual incomes, after payment of all taxes, should be limited effectively by further taxation to a maximum net income of $25,000 a year. And it is equally important that corporate profits should not exceed a reasonable amount in any case.

The nation must have more money to run the war. People must stop spending for luxuries. Our country needs a far greater share of our incomes.

For this is a global war, and it will cost this nation nearly one hundred billion dollars in 1943.

In that global war there are now four main areas of combat; and I should like to speak briefly of them, not in the order of their importance, for all of them are vital and all of them are interrelated.

1. The Russian front. Here the Germans are still unable to gain the smashing victory which, almost a year ago, Hitler announced he had already achieved. Germany has been able to capture important Russian territory. Nevertheless, Hitler has been unable to destroy a single Russian Army; and this, you may be sure, has been, and still is, his main objective. Millions of German troops seem doomed to spend another cruel and bitter winter on the Russian front. Yes, the Russians are killing more Nazis, and destroying more airplanes and tanks than are being smashed on any other front. They are fighting not only bravely but brilliantly. In spite of any setbacks Russia will hold out, and with the help of her Allies will ultimately drive every Nazi from her soil.

2. The Pacific Ocean Area. This area must be grouped together as a whole—every part of it, land and sea. We have stopped one major Japanese offensive; and we have inflicted heavy losses on their fleet. But they still possess great strength; they seek to keep the initiative; and they will undoubtedly strike hard again. We must not overrate the importance of our successes in the Solomon Islands, though we may be proud of the skill with which these local operations were conducted. At the same time, we need not underrate the significance of our victory at Midway. There we stopped the major Japanese offensive.

3. In the Mediterranean and the Middle East area the British, together with the South Africans, Australians, New Zealanders, Indian troops and others of the United Nations, including ourselves, are fighting a desperate battle with the Germans and Italians. The Axis powers are fighting to gain control of that area, dominate the Mediterranean and the Indian Ocean, and gain contact with the Japanese Navy. The battle in the Middle East is now joined. We are well aware of our danger, but we are hopeful of the outcome.

4. The European area. Here the aim is an offensive against Germany. There are at least a dozen different points at which attacks can be launched. You, of course, do not expect me to give details of future plans, but you can

rest assured that preparations are being made here and in Britain toward this purpose. The power of Germany must be broken on the battlefields of Europe.

Various people urge that we concentrate our forces on one or another of these four areas, although no one suggests that any one of the four areas should be abandoned. Certainly, it could not be seriously urged that we abandon aid to Russia, or that we surrender all of the Pacific to Japan, or the Mediterranean and Middle East to Germany, or give up an offensive against Germany. The American people may be sure that we shall neglect none of the four great theaters of war.

Certain vital military decisions have been made. In due time you will know what these decisions are—and so will our enemies. I can say now that all of these decisions are directed toward taking the offensive.

Today, exactly nine months after Pearl Harbor, we have sent overseas three times more men than we transported to France in the first nine months of the first World War. We have done this in spite of greater danger and fewer ships. And every week sees a gain in the actual number of American men and weapons in the fighting areas. These reinforcements in men and munitions are continuing, and will continue to go forward.

This war will finally be won by the coordination of all the armies, navies and air forces of all of the United Nations operating in unison against our enemies.

This will require vast assemblies of weapons and men at all the vital points of attack. We and our allies have worked for years to achieve superiority in weapons. We have no doubts about the superiority of our men. We glory in the individual exploits of our soldiers, our sailors, our marines, our merchant seamen. Lieutenant John James Powers was one of these—and there are thousands of others in the forces of the United Nations.

Several thousand Americans have met death in battle. Other thousands will lose their lives. But many millions stand ready to step into their places—to engage in a struggle to the very death. For they know that the enemy is determined to destroy us, our homes and our institutions—that in this war it is kill or be killed.

Battles are not won by soldiers or sailors who think first of their own personal safety. And wars are not won by people who are concerned primarily with their own comfort, their own convenience, their own pocketbooks.

We Americans of today bear the gravest of responsibilities. And all of the United Nations share them.

All of us here at home are being tested—for our fortitude, for our selfless devotion to our country and to our cause.

This is the toughest war of all time. We need not leave it to historians of the future to answer the question whether we are tough enough to meet this unprecedented challenge. We can give that answer now. The answer is "Yes."

October 12, 1942.

My Fellow Americans:

As you know, I have recently come back from a trip of inspection of camps and training stations and war factories.

The main thing that I observed on this trip is not exactly news. It is the plain fact that the American people are united as never before in their determination to do a job and to do it well.

This whole nation of 130,000,000 free men, women and children is becoming one great fighting force. Some of us are soldiers or sailors, some of us are civilians. Some of us are fighting the war in airplanes five miles above the continent of Europe or the islands of the Pacific—and some of us are fighting it in mines deep down in the earth of Pennsylvania or Montana. A few of us are decorated with medals for heroic achievement, but all of us can have that deep and permanent inner satisfaction that comes from doing the best we know how—each of us playing an honorable part in the great struggle to save our democratic civilization.

Whatever our individual circumstances or opportunities—we are all in it, and our spirit is good, and we Americans and our allies are going to win—and do not let anyone tell you anything different.

That is the main thing that I saw on my trip around the country—unbeatable spirit. If the leaders of Germany and Japan could have come along with me, and had seen what I saw, they would agree with my conclusions. Unfortunately, they were unable to make the trip with me. And that is one reason why we are carrying our war effort overseas—to them.

With every passing week the war increases in scope and intensity. That is true in Europe, in Africa, in Asia, and on all the seas.

The strength of the United Nations is on the upgrade in this war. The Axis leaders, on the other hand, know by now that they have already reached their full strength, and that their steadily mounting losses in men and material cannot be fully replaced. Germany and Japan are already realizing what the inevitable result will be when the total strength of the United Nations hits them—at additional places on the earth's surface.

One of the principal weapons of our enemies in the past has been their use of what is called "The War of Nerves." They have spread falsehood and terror; they have started Fifth Columns everywhere; they have duped the innocent; they have fomented suspicion and hate between neighbors; they have aided and abetted those people in other nations—including our own—whose words and deeds are advertised from Berlin and from Tokyo as proof of our disunity.

The greatest defense against all such propaganda, of course, is the common sense of the common people—and that defense is prevailing.

The "War of Nerves" against the United Nations is now turning into a boomerang. For the first time, the Nazi propaganda machine is on the defensive. They begin to apologize to their own people for the repulse of their vast forces at Stalingrad, and for the enormous casualties they are suffering. They are compelled to beg their overworked people to rally their weakened production. They even publicly admit, for the first time, that Germany can be fed only at the cost of stealing food from the rest of Europe.

They are proclaiming that a second front is impossible; but, at the same time, they are desperately rushing troops in all directions, and stringing barbed wire all the way from the coasts of Finland and Norway to the islands of the Eastern Mediterranean.

Meanwhile, they are driven to increase the fury of their atrocities.

The United Nations have decided to establish the identity of those Nazi leaders who are responsible for the innumerable acts of savagery. As each of these criminal deeds is committed, it is being carefully investigated; and the evidence is being relentlessly piled up for the future purposes of justice.

We have made it entirely clear that the United Nations seek no mass reprisals against the populations of Germany or Italy or Japan. But the ring leaders and their brutal henchmen must be named, and apprehended, and tried in accordance with the judicial processes of criminal law.

There are now millions of Americans in army camps, in naval stations, in factories and in shipyards.

Who are these millions upon whom the life of our country depends? What are they thinking? What are their doubts? What are their hopes? And how is the work progressing?

The Commander-in-Chief cannot learn all of the answers to these questions in Washington. And that is why I made the trip I did.

It is very easy to say, as some have said, that when the President travels through the country he should go with a blare of trumpets, with crowds on the sidewalks, with batteries of reporters and photographers—talking and posing with all of the politicians of the land.

But having had some experience in this war and in the last war, I can tell you very simply that the kind of trip I took permitted me to concentrate on the work I had to do without expending time, meeting all the demands of publicity. And—I might add—it was a particular pleasure to make a tour of the country without having to give a single thought to politics.

I expect to make other trips for similar purposes, and I shall make them in the same way.

In the last war, I had seen great factories; but until I saw some of the new present-day plants, I had not thoroughly visualized our American war effort. Of course, I saw only a small portion of all our plants, but that portion was a good cross-section, and it was deeply impressive.

The United States has been at war for only ten months, and is engaged in the enormous task of multiplying its armed forces many times. We are by no means at full production level yet. But I could not help asking myself on the trip, where would we be today if the government of the United States had not begun to build many of its factories for this huge increase more than two years ago, more than a year before war was forced upon us at Pearl Harbor?

We have also had to face the problem of shipping. Ships in every part of the world continue to be sunk by enemy action. But the total tonnage of ships coming out of American, Canadian and British shipyards, day by day, has increased so fast that we are getting ahead of our enemies in the bitter battle of transportation.

In expanding our shipping, we have had to enlist many thousands of men for our Merchant Marine. These men are serving magnificently. They are risking their lives every hour so that guns and tanks and planes and ammunition and food may be carried to the heroic defenders of Stalingrad and to all the United Nations' forces all over the world.

A few days ago I awarded the first Maritime Distinguished Service Medal to a young man—Edward F. Cheney of Yeadon, Pennsylvania—who had shown great gallantry in rescuing his comrades from the oily waters of the sea after their ship had been torpedoed. There will be many more such acts of bravery.

In one sense my recent trip was a hurried one, out through the Middle West, to the Northwest, down the length of the Pacific Coast and back through the Southwest and the South. In another sense, however, it was a leisurely trip, because I had the opportunity to talk to the people who are actually doing the work—management and labor alike—on their own home grounds. And it gave me a fine chance to do some thinking about the major problems of our war effort on the basis of first things first.

As I told the three press association representatives who accompanied me, I was impressed by the large proportion of women employed—doing skilled manual labor running machines. As time goes on, and many more of our men enter the armed forces, this proportion of women will increase. Within less than a year from now, I think, there will probably be as many women as men working in our war production plants.

I had some enlightening experiences relating to the old saying of us men that curiosity—inquisitiveness—is stronger among woman. I noticed, frequently, that when we drove unannounced down the middle aisle of a great plant full of workers and machines, the first people to look up from their work were the men—and not the women. It was chiefly the men who were arguing as to whether that fellow in the straw hat was really the President or not.

So having seen the quality of the work and of the workers on our production lines—and coupling these firsthand observations with the reports of actual performance of our weapons on the fighting fronts—I can say to you that we are getting ahead of our enemies in the battle of production.

And of great importance to our future production was the effective and rapid manner in which the Congress met the serious problem of the rising cost of living. It was a splendid example of the operation of democratic processes in wartime.

The machinery to carry out this act of the Congress was put into effect within twelve hours after the bill was signed. The legislation will help the cost-of-living problems of every worker in every factory and on every farm in the land.

In order to keep stepping up our production, we have had to add millions of workers to the total labor force of the nation. And as new factories came into operation, we must find additional millions of workers.

This presents a formidable problem in the mobilization of manpower.

It is not that we do not have enough people in this country to do the job. The problem is to have the right numbers of the right people in the right places at the right time.

We are learning to ration materials, and we must now learn to ration manpower. The major objectives of a sound manpower policy are:

First, to select and train men of the highest fighting efficiency needed for our armed forces in the achievement of victory over our enemies in combat.

Second, to man our war industries and farms with the workers needed to produce the arms and munitions and food required by ourselves and by our fighting allies to win this war.

In order to do this, we shall be compelled to stop workers from moving from one war job to another as a matter of personal preference; to stop employers from stealing labor from each other; to use older men, and handicapped people, and more women, and even grown boys and girls, wherever possible and reasonable, to replace men of military age and fitness; to train new personnel for essential war work; and to stop the wastage of labor in all non- essential activities.

There are many other things that we can do, and do immediately, to help meet this manpower problem.

The school authorities in all the states should work out plans to enable our high school students to take some time from their school year, and to use their summer vacations, to help farmers raise and harvest their crops, or to work somewhere in the war industries. This does not mean closing schools and stopping education. It does mean giving older students a better opportunity to contribute their bit to the war effort. Such work will do no harm to the students.

People should do their work as near their homes as possible. We cannot afford to transport a single worker into an area where there is already a worker available to do the job.

In some communities, employers dislike to employ women. In others they are reluctant to hire Negroes. In still others, older men are not wanted. We can no longer afford to indulge such prejudices or practices.

Every citizen wants to know what essential war work he can do the best. He can get the answer by applying to the nearest United States Employment Service office. There are four thousand five hundred of these offices throughout the nation. They form the corner grocery stores of our manpower system. This network of employment offices is prepared to advise every citizen where his skills and labors are needed most, and to refer him to an employer who can utilize them to best advantage in the war effort.

Perhaps the most difficult phase of the manpower problem is the scarcity of farm labor in many places. I have seen evidences of the fact, however, that the people are trying to meet it as well as possible.

In one community that I visited a perishable crop was harvested by turning out the whole of the high school for three or four days.

And in another community of fruit growers the usual Japanese labor was not available; but when the fruit ripened, the banker, the butcher, the lawyer, the garage man, the druggist, the local editor, and in fact every able-bodied man and woman in the town, left their occupations and went out, gathered the fruit, and sent it to market.

Every farmer in the land must realize fully that his production is part of war production, and that he is regarded by the nation as essential to victory. The American people expect him to keep his production up, and even to increase it. We will use every effort to help him to get labor; but, at the same time, he and the people of his community must use ingenuity and cooperative effort to produce crops, and livestock and dairy products.

It may be that all of our volunteer effort—however well intentioned and well administered—will not suffice wholly to solve this problem. In that case, we shall have to adopt new legislation. And if this is necessary, I do not believe that the American people will shrink from it.

In a sense, every American, because of the privilege of his citizenship, is a part of the Selective Service.

The Nation owes a debt of gratitude to the Selective Service boards. The successful operation of the Selective Service System and the way it has been accepted by the great mass of our citizens give us confidence that if necessary, the same principle could be used to solve any manpower problem.

And I want to say also a word of praise and thanks to the more than ten million people, all over the country, who have volunteered for the work of civilian defense—and who are working hard at it. They are displaying unselfish devotion in the patient performance of their often tiresome and always anonymous tasks. In doing this important neighborly work they are helping to fortify our national unity and our real understanding of the fact that we are all involved in this war.

Naturally, on my trip I was most interested in watching the training of our fighting forces.

All of our combat units that go overseas must consist of young, strong men who have had thorough training. An Army division that has an average age of twenty-three or twenty-four is a better fighting unit than one which has an average age of thirty-three or thirty-four. The more of such troops we have in the field, the sooner the war will be won, and the smaller will be the cost in casualties.

Therefore, I believe that it will be necessary to lower the present minimum age limit for Selective Service from twenty years down to eighteen. We have learned how inevitable that is—and how important to the speeding up of victory.

I can very thoroughly understand the feelings of all parents whose sons have entered our armed forces. I have an appreciation of that feeling and so has my wife.

I want every father and every mother who has a son in the service to know—again, from what I have seen with my own eyes—that the men in the Army, Navy and Marine Corps are receiving today the best possible training, equipment and medical care. And we will never fail to provide for the spiritual needs of our officers and men under the Chaplains of our armed services.

Good training will save many, many lives in battle. The highest rate of casualties is always suffered by units comprised of inadequately trained men.

We can be sure that the combat units of our Army and Navy are well manned, well equipped, and well trained. Their effectiveness in action will depend upon the quality of their leadership, and upon the wisdom of the strategic plans on which all military operations are based.

I can say one thing about these plans of ours: They are not being decided by the typewriter strategists who expound their views on the radio or in the press.

One of the greatest of American soldiers, Robert E. Lee, once remarked on the tragic fact that in the war of his day all of the best generals were apparently working on newspapers instead of in the Army. And that seems to be true in all wars.

The trouble with the typewriter strategists is that while they may be full of bright ideas, they are not in possession of much information about the facts or problems of military operations.

We, therefore, will continue to leave the plans for this war to the military leaders.

The military and naval plans of the United States are made by the Joint Staff of the Army and Navy which is constantly in session in Washington. The Chiefs of this Staff are Admiral Leahy, General Marshall, Admiral King and General Arnold. They meet and confer regularly with representatives of the British Joint Staff, and with representatives of Russia, China, the Netherlands, Poland, Norway, the British Dominions and other nations working in the common cause.

Since this unity of operations was put into effect last January, there has been a very substantial agreement between these planners, all of whom are trained in the profession of arms—air, sea and land—from their early years. As Commander-in-Chief I have at all times also been in substantial agreement.

As I have said before, many major decisions of strategy have been made. One of them—on which we have all agreed—relates to the necessity of diverting enemy forces from Russia and China to other theaters of war by new offensives against Germany and Japan. An announcement of how these offensives are to be launched, and when, and where, cannot be broadcast over the radio at this time.

We are celebrating today the exploit of a bold and adventurous Italian—Christopher Columbus—who with the aid of Spain opened up a new world where freedom and tolerance and respect for human rights and dignity provided an asylum for the oppressed of the Old World.

Today, the sons of the New World are fighting in lands far distant from their own America. They are fighting to save for all mankind, including ourselves, the principles which have flourished in this new world of freedom.

We are mindful of the countless millions of people whose future liberty and whose very lives depend upon permanent victory for the United Nations.

There are a few people in this country who, when the collapse of the Axis begins, will tell our people that we are safe once more; that we can tell the rest of the world to "stew in its own juice"; that never again will we help to pull "the other fellow's chestnuts from the fire"; that the future of civilization can jolly well take care of itself insofar as we are concerned.

But it is useless to win battles if the cause for which we fight these battles is lost. It is useless to win a war unless it stays won.

We, therefore, fight for the restoration and perpetuation of faith and hope and peace throughout the world.

The objective of today is clear and realistic. It is to destroy completely the military power of Germany, Italy and Japan to such good purpose that their threat against us and all the other United Nations cannot be revived a generation hence.

We are united in seeking the kind of victory that will guarantee that our grandchildren can grow and, under God, may live their lives, free from the constant threat of invasion, destruction, slavery and violent death.

May 2, 1943.

My Fellow Americans:

I am speaking tonight to the American people, and in particular to those of our citizens who are coal miners.

Tonight this country faces a serious crisis. We are engaged in a war on the successful outcome of which will depend the whole future of our country.

This war has reached a new critical phase. After the years that we have spent in preparation, we have moved into active and continuing battle with our enemies. We are pouring into the world-wide conflict everything that we have—our young men, and the vast resources of our nation.

I have just returned from a two weeks' tour of inspection on which I saw our men being trained and our war materials made. My trip took me through twenty states. I saw thousands of workers on the production line, making airplanes, and guns and ammunition.

Everywhere I found great eagerness to get on with the war. Men and women are working long hours at difficult jobs and living under difficult conditions without complaint.

Along thousands of miles of track I saw countless acres of newly ploughed fields. The farmers of this country are planting the crops that are needed to feed our armed forces, our civilian population and our Allies. Those crops will be harvested.

On my trip, I saw hundreds of thousands of soldiers. Young men who were green recruits last autumn have matured into self-assured and hardened fighting men. They are in splendid physical condition. They are mastering the superior weapons that we are pouring out of our factories.

The American people have accomplished a miracle.

However, all of our massed effort is none too great to meet the demands of this war. We shall need everything that we have and everything that our Allies have to defeat the Nazis and the Fascists in the coming battles on the continent of Europe, and the Japanese on the continent of Asia and in the islands of the Pacific.

This tremendous forward movement of the United States and the United Nations cannot be stopped by our enemies.

And equally, it must not be hampered by any one individual or by the leaders of any one group here back home.

I want to make it clear that every American coal miner who has stopped mining coal—no matter how sincere his motives, no matter how legitimate he may believe his grievances to be—every idle miner directly and individually is obstructing our war effort. We have not yet won this war. We will win this war only as we produce and deliver our total American effort on the high seas and on the battle fronts. And that requires unrelenting, uninterrupted effort here on the home front.

A stopping of the coal supply, even for a short time, would involve a gamble with the lives of American soldiers and sailors and the future security of our whole people. It would involve an unwarranted, unnecessary and terribly dangerous gamble with our chances for victory.

Therefore, I say to all miners—and to all Americans everywhere, at home and abroad—the production of coal will not be stopped.

Tonight, I am speaking to the essential patriotism of the miners, and to the patriotism of their wives and children. And I am going to state the true facts of this case as simply and as plainly as I know how.

After the attack at Pearl Harbor, the three great labor organizations—the American Federation of Labor, the Congress of Industrial Organizations, and the Railroad Brotherhoods—gave the positive assurance that there would be no strikes as long as the war lasted. And the President of the United Mine workers of America was a party to that assurance.

That pledge was applauded throughout the country. It was a forcible means of telling the world that we Americans—135,000,000 of us—are united in our determination to fight this total war with our total will and our total power.

At the request of employers and of organized labor—including the United Mine Workers—the War Labor Board was set up for settling any disputes which could not be adjusted through collective bargaining. The War Labor Board is a tribunal on which workers, employers and the general public are equally represented.

In the present coal crisis, conciliation and mediation were tried unsuccessfully.

In accordance with the law, the case was then certified to the War Labor Board, the agency created for this express purpose with the approval of organized labor. The members of the Board followed the usual practice which has proved successful in other disputes. Acting promptly, they undertook to get all the facts of this case from both the miners and the operators.

The national officers of the United Mine Workers, however, declined to have anything to do with the fact-finding of the War Labor Board. The only excuse that they offer is that the War Labor Board is prejudiced.

The War Labor Board has been and is ready to give this case a fair and impartial hearing. And I have given my assurance that if any adjustment of wages is made by the Board, it will be made retroactive to April first. But the national officers of the United Mine Workers refused to participate in the hearing, when asked to do so last Monday.

On Wednesday of this past week, while the Board was proceeding with the case, stoppages began to occur in some mines. On Thursday morning I telegraphed to the officers of the United Mine Workers asking that the miners continue mining coal on Saturday morning. However, a general strike throughout the industry became effective on Friday night.

The responsibility for the crisis that we now face rests squarely on these national officers of the United Mine Workers, and not on the government of the United States. But the consequences of this arbitrary action threaten all of us everywhere.

At ten o'clock yesterday morning the government took over the mines. I called upon the miners to return to work for their government. The government needs their services just as surely as it needs the services of our soldiers, and sailors, and marines—and the services of the millions who are turning out the munitions of war.

You miners have sons in the Army and Navy and Marine Corps. You have sons who at this very minute—this split second—may be fighting in New Guinea, or in the Aleutian Islands, or Guadalcanal, or Tunisia, or China, or protecting troop ships and supplies against submarines on the high seas. We have already received telegrams from some of our fighting men overseas, and I only wish they could tell you what they think of the stoppage of work in the coal mines.

Some of your own sons have come back from the fighting fronts, wounded. A number of them, for example, are now here in an Army hospital in Washington. Several of them have been decorated by their government.

I could tell you of one from Pennsylvania. He was a coal miner before his induction, and his father is a coal miner. He was seriously wounded by Nazi machine gun bullets while he was on a bombing mission over Europe in a Flying Fortress.

Another boy, from Kentucky, the son of a coal miner, was wounded when our troops first landed in North Africa six months ago.

There is still another, from Illinois. He was a coal miner—his father and two brothers are coal miners. He was seriously wounded in Tunisia while attempting to rescue two comrades whose jeep had been blown up by a Nazi mine.

These men do not consider themselves heroes. They would probably be embarrassed if I mentioned their names over the air. They were wounded in the line of duty. They know how essential it is to the tens of thousands—hundreds of thousands—and ultimately millions of other young Americans to get the best of arms and equipment into the hands of our fighting forces—and get them there quickly.

The fathers and mothers of our fighting men, their brothers and sisters and friends—and that includes all of us—are also in the line of duty—the production line. Any failure in production may well result in costly defeat on the field of battle.

There can be no one among us—no one faction powerful enough to interrupt the forward march of our people to victory.

You miners have ample reason to know that there are certain basic rights for which this country stands, and that those rights are worth fighting for and worth dying for. That is why you have sent your sons and brothers from every mining town in the nation to join in the great struggle overseas. That is why you have contributed so generously, so willingly, to the purchase of war bonds and to the many funds for the relief of war victims in foreign lands. That is why, since this war was started in 1939, you have increased the annual production of coal by almost two hundred million tons a year.

The toughness of your sons in our armed forces is not surprising. They come of fine, rugged stock. Men who work in the mines are not unaccustomed to hardship. It has been the objective of this government to reduce that hardship, to obtain for miners and for all who do the nation's work a better standard of living.

I know only too well that the cost of living is troubling the miners' families, and troubling the families of millions of other workers throughout the country as well.

A year ago it became evident to all of us that something had to be done about living costs. Your government determined not to let the cost of living continue to go up as it did in the first World War.

Your government has been determined to maintain stability of both prices and wages—so that a dollar would buy, so far as possible, the same amount of the necessities of life. And by necessities I mean just that—not the luxuries, not the fancy goods that we have learned to do without in wartime.

So far, we have not been able to keep the prices of some necessities as low as we should have liked to keep them. That is true not only in coal towns but in many other places.

Wherever we find that prices of essentials have risen too high, they will be brought down. Wherever we find that price ceilings are being violated, the violators will be punished.

Rents have been fixed in most parts of the country. In many cities they have been cut to below where they were before we entered the war. Clothing prices have generally remained stable.

These two items make up more than a third of the total budget of the worker's family.

As for food, which today accounts for about another third of the family expenditure on the average, I want to repeat again: your government will continue to take all necessary measures to eliminate unjustified and avoidable price increases. And we are today taking measures to "roll back" the prices of meats.

The war is going to go on. Coal will be mined no matter what any individual thinks about it. The operation of our factories, our power plants, our railroads will not be stopped. Our munitions must move to our troops.

And so, under these circumstances, it is inconceivable that any patriotic miner can choose any course other than going back to work and mining coal.

The nation cannot afford violence of any kind at the coal mines or in coal towns. I have placed authority for the resumption of coal mining in the hands of a civilian, the Secretary of the Interior. If it becomes necessary to protect any miner who seeks patriotically to go back and work, then that miner must have and his family must have—and will have—complete and adequate protection. If it becomes necessary to have troops at the mine mouths or in coal towns for the protection of working miners and their families, those troops will be doing police duty for the sake of the nation as a whole, and particularly for the sake of the fighting men in the Army, the Navy and the Marines—your sons and mine—who are fighting our common enemies all over the world.

I understand the devotion of the coal miners to their union. I know of the sacrifices they have made to build it up. I believe now, as I have all my life, in the right of workers to join unions and to protect their unions. I want to make it absolutely clear that this government is not going to do anything now to weaken those rights in the coal fields.

Every improvement in the conditions of the coal miners of this country has had my hearty support, and I do not mean to desert them now. But I also do not mean to desert my obligations and responsibilities as President of the United States and Commander- in-Chief of the Army and Navy.

The first necessity is the resumption of coal mining. The terms of the old contract will be followed by the Secretary of the Interior. If an adjustment in wages results from a decision of the War Labor Board, or from any new agreement between the operators and miners, which is approved by the War Labor Board, that adjustment will be made retroactive to April first.

In the message that I delivered to the Congress four months ago, I expressed my conviction that the spirit of this nation is good.

Since then, I have seen our troops in the Caribbean area, in bases on the coasts of our ally, Brazil, and in North Africa. Recently I have again seen great numbers of our fellow countrymen—soldiers and civilians—from the Atlantic Seaboard to the Mexican border and to the Rocky Mountains.

Tonight, in the fact of a crisis of serious proportions in the coal industry, I say again that the spirit or this nation is good. I know that the American people will not tolerate any threat offered to their government by anyone. I believe the coal miners will not continue the strike against their government. I believe that the coal miners as Americans will not fail to heed the clear call to duty. Like all other good Americans, they will march shoulder to shoulder with their armed forces to victory.

Tomorrow the Stars and Stripes will fly over the coal mines, and I hope that every miner will be at work under that flag.

July 28, 1943.

My Fellow Americans:

Over a year and a half ago I said this to the Congress: "The militarists in Berlin, and Rome and Tokyo started this war, but the massed angered forces of common humanity will finish it."

Today that prophecy is in the process of being fulfilled. The massed, angered forces of common humanity are on the march. They are going forward—on the Russian front, in the vast Pacific area, and into Europe—converging upon their ultimate objectives: Berlin and Tokyo.

I think the first crack in the Axis has come. The criminal, corrupt Fascist regime in Italy is going to pieces.

The pirate philosophy of the Fascists and the Nazis cannot stand adversity. The military superiority of the United Nations—on sea and land, and in the air—has been applied in the right place and at the right time.

Hitler refused to send sufficient help to save Mussolini. In fact, Hitler's troops in Sicily stole the Italians' motor equipment, leaving Italian soldiers so stranded that they had no choice but to surrender. Once again the Germans betrayed their Italian allies, as they had done time and time again on the Russian front and in the long retreat from Egypt, through Libya and Tripoli, to the final surrender in Tunisia.

And so Mussolini came to the reluctant conclusion that the "jig was up"; he could see the shadow of the long arm of justice.

But he and his Fascist gang will be brought to book, and punished for their crimes against humanity. No criminal will be allowed to escape by the expedient of "resignation."

So our terms to Italy are still the same as our terms to Germany and Japan—"unconditional surrender."

We will have no truck with Fascism in any way, in any shape or manner. We will permit no vestige of Fascism to remain.

Eventually Italy will reconstitute herself. It will be the people of Italy who will do that, choosing their own government in accordance with the basic democratic principles of liberty and equality. In the meantime, the United Nations will not follow the pattern set by Mussolini and Hitler and the Japanese for the treatment of occupied countries—the pattern of pillage and starvation.

We are already helping the Italian people in Sicily. With their cordial cooperation, we are establishing and maintaining security and order—we are dissolving the organizations which have kept them under Fascist tyranny—we are providing them with the necessities of life until the time comes when they can fully provide for themselves.

Indeed, the people in Sicily today are rejoicing in the fact that for the first time in years they are permitted to enjoy the fruits of their own labors—they can eat what they themselves grow, instead of having it stolen from them by the Fascists and the Nazis.

In every country conquered by the Nazis and the Fascists, or the Japanese militarists, the people have been reduced to the status of slaves or chattels.

It is our determination to restore these conquered peoples to the dignity of human beings, masters of their own fate, entitled to freedom of speech, freedom of religion, freedom from want, and freedom from fear.

We have started to make good on that promise.

I am sorry if I step on the toes of those Americans who, playing party politics at home, call that kind of foreign policy "crazy altruism "and "starry-eyed dreaming."

Meanwhile, the war in Sicily and Italy goes on. It must go on, and will go on, until the Italian people realize the futility of continuing to fight in a lost cause—a cause to which the people of Italy never gave their wholehearted approval and support.

It is a little over a year since we planned the North African campaign. It is six months since we planned the Sicilian campaign. I confess that I am of an impatient disposition, but I think that I understand and that most people understand the amount of time necessary to prepare for any major military or naval operation. We cannot just pick up the telephone and order a new campaign to start the next week.

For example, behind the invasion forces in North Africa, the invasion forces that went out of North Africa, were thousands of ships and planes guarding the long, perilous sea lanes, carrying the men, carrying the equipment and the supplies to the point of attack. And behind all these were the railroad lines and the highways here back home that carried the men and the munitions to the ports of embarkation—there were the factories and the mines and the farms here back home that turned out the materials—there were the training camps here back home where the men learned how to perform the strange and difficult and dangerous tasks which were to meet them on the beaches and in the deserts and in the mountains.

All this had to be repeated, first in North Africa and then in the attack on Sicily. Here the factor—in Sicily—the factor of air attack was added—for we could use North Africa as the base for softening up the landing places and lines of defense in Sicily, and the lines of supply in Italy.

It is interesting for us to realize that every flying fortress that bombed harbor installations at, for example, Naples, from its base in North Africa required 1,110 gallons of gasoline for each single mission, and that this is the equal of about 375 "A" ration tickets—enough gas to drive your car five times across this continent. You will better understand your part in the war—and what gasoline rationing means—if you multiply this by the gasoline needs of thousands of planes and hundreds of thousands of jeeps, and trucks and tanks that are now serving overseas.

I think that the personal convenience of the individual, or the individual family back home here in the United States will appear somewhat less important when I tell you that the initial assault force on Sicily involved 3,000 ships which carried 160,000 men—Americans, British, Canadians and French—together with 14,000 vehicles, 600 tanks, and 1,800 guns. And this initial force was followed every day and every night by thousands of reinforcements.

The meticulous care with which the operation in Sicily was planned has paid dividends. Our casualties in men, in ships and material have been low—in fact, far below our estimate.

And all of us are proud of the superb skill and courage of the officers and men who have conducted and are conducting those operations. The toughest resistance developed on the front of the British Eighth Army, which included the Canadians. But that is no new experience for that magnificent fighting force which has made the Germans pay a heavy price for each hour of delay in the final victory. The American Seventh Army, after a stormy landing on the exposed beaches of southern Sicily, swept with record speed across the island into the capital at Palermo. For many of our troops this was their first battle experience, but they have carried themselves like veterans.

And we must give credit for the coordination of the diverse forces in the field, and for the planning of the whole campaign, to the wise and skillful leadership of General Eisenhower. Admiral Cunningham, General Alexander and Sir Marshal Tedder have been towers of strength in handling the complex details of naval and ground and air activities.

You have heard some people say that the British and the Americans can never get along well together—you have heard some people say that the Army and the Navy and the Air Forces can never get along well together—that real cooperation between them is impossible. Tunisia and Sicily have given the lie, once and for all, to these narrow-minded prejudices.

The dauntless fighting spirit of the British people in this war has been expressed in the historic words and deeds of Winston Churchill—and the world knows how the American people feel about him.

Ahead of us are much bigger fights. We and our Allies will go into them as we went into Sicily—together. And we shall carry on together.

Today our production of ships is almost unbelievable. This year we are producing over nineteen million tons of merchant shipping and next year our production will be over twenty-one million tons. And in addition to our shipments across the Atlantic, we must realize that in this war we are operating in the Aleutians, in the distant parts of the Southwest Pacific, in India, and off the shores of South America.

For several months we have been losing fewer ships by sinkings, and we have been destroying more and more U-boats. We hope this will continue. But we cannot be sure. We must not lower our guard for one single instant.

One tangible result of our great increase in merchant shipping—which I think will be good news to civilians at home—is that tonight we are able to terminate the rationing of coffee. We also expect that within a short time we shall get greatly increased allowances of sugar.

Those few Americans who grouse and complain about the inconveniences of life here in the United States should learn some lessons from the civilian populations of our Allies—Britain, and China, and Russia—and of all the lands occupied by our common enemy.

The heaviest and most decisive fighting today is going on in Russia. I am glad that the British and we have been able to contribute somewhat to the great striking power of the Russian armies.

In 1941-1942 the Russians were able to retire without breaking, to move many of their war plants from western Russia far into the interior, to stand together with complete unanimity in the defense of their homeland.

The success of the Russian armies has shown that it is dangerous to make prophecies about them—a fact which has been forcibly brought home to that mystic master of strategic intuition, Herr Hitler.

The short-lived German offensive, launched early this month, was a desperate attempt to bolster the morale of the German people. The Russians were not fooled by this. They went ahead with their own plans for attack—plans which coordinate with the whole United Nations' offensive strategy.

The world has never seen greater devotion, determination and self- sacrifice than have been displayed by the Russian people and their armies, under the leadership of Marshal Joseph Stalin.

With a nation which in saving itself is thereby helping to save all the world from the Nazi menace, this country of ours should always be glad to be a good neighbor and a sincere friend in the world of the future.

In the Pacific, we are pushing the Japs around from the Aleutians to New Guinea. There too we have taken the initiative—and we are not going to let go of it.

It becomes clearer and clearer that the attrition, the whittling down process against the Japanese is working. The Japs have lost more planes and more ships than they have been able to replace.

The continuous and energetic prosecution of the war of attrition will drive the Japs back from their over-extended line running from Burma and Siam and the Straits Settlement through the Netherlands Indies to eastern New Guinea and the Solomons. And we have good reason to believe that their shipping and their air power cannot support such outposts.

Our naval and land and air strength in the Pacific is constantly growing. And if the Japanese are basing their future plans for the Pacific on a long period in which they will be permitted to consolidate and exploit their conquered resources, they had better start revising their plans now. I give that to them merely as a helpful suggestion.

We are delivering planes and vital war supplies for the heroic armies of Generalissimo Chiang Sai-shek, and we must do more at all costs.

Our air supply line from India to China across enemy territory continues despite attempted Japanese interference. We have seized the initiative from the Japanese in the air over Burma and now we enjoy superiority. We are bombing Japanese communications, supply dumps, and bases in China, in Indo-China, in Burma.

But we are still far from our main objectives in the war against Japan. Let us remember, however, how far we were a year ago from any of our objectives in the European theatre. We are pushing forward to occupation of positions which in time will enable us to attack the Japanese Islands themselves from the North, from the South, from the East, and from the West.

You have heard it said that while we are succeeding greatly on the fighting front, we are failing miserably on the home front. I think this is another of those immaturities—a false slogan easy to state but untrue in the essential facts.

For the longer this war goes on the clearer it becomes that no one can draw a blue pencil down the middle of a page and call one side "the fighting front" and the other side "the home front." For the two of them are inexorably tied together.

Every combat division, every naval task force, every squadron of fighting planes is dependent for its equipment and ammunition and fuel and food, as indeed it is for its manpower, dependent on the American people in civilian clothes in the offices and in the factories and on the farms at home.

The same kind of careful planning that gained victory in North Africa and Sicily is required, if we are to make victory an enduring reality and do our share in building the kind of peaceful world that will justify the sacrifices made in this war.

The United Nations are substantially agreed on the general objectives for the post-war world. They are also agreed that this is not the time to engage in an international discussion of *all* the terms of peace and *all* the details of the future. Let us win the war first. We must not relax our pressure on the enemy by taking time out to define every boundary and settle every political controversy in every part of the world. The important thing—the all-important thing now is to get on with the war—and to win it.

While concentrating on military victory, we are not neglecting the planning of the things to come, the freedoms which we know will make for more decency and greater justice throughout the world.

Among many other things we are, today, laying plans for the return to civilian life of our gallant men and women in the armed services. They must not be demobilized into an environment of inflation and unemployment, to a place on a bread line, or on a corner selling apples. We must, this time, have plans ready—instead of waiting to do a hasty, inefficient, and ill-considered job at the last moment.

I have assured our men in the armed forces that the American people would not let them down when the war is won.

I hope that the Congress will help in carrying out this assurance, for obviously the executive branch of the government cannot do it alone. May the Congress do its duty in this regard. The American people will insist on fulfilling this American obligation to the men and women in the armed forces who are winning this war for us.

Of course, the returning soldier and sailor and marine are a part of the problem of demobilizing the rest of the millions of Americans who have been working and living in a war economy since 1941. That larger objective of reconverting wartime America to a peacetime basis is one for which your government is laying plans to be submitted to the Congress for action.

But the members of the armed forces have been compelled to make greater economic sacrifice and every other kind of sacrifice than the rest of us, and they are entitled to definite action to help take care of their special problems.

The least to which they are entitled, it seems to me, is something like this:

First, mustering-out pay to every member of the armed forces and merchant marine when he or she is honorably discharged; mustering- out pay large enough in each case to cover a reasonable period of time between his discharge and the finding of a new job.

Second, in case no job is found after diligent search, then unemployment insurance if the individual registers with the United States Employment Service.

Third, an opportunity for members of the armed services to get further education or trade training at the cost of the government.

Fourth, allowance of credit to all members of the armed forces, under unemployment compensation and federal old-age and survivors' insurance, for their period of service. For these purposes they ought to be treated as if they had continued their employment in private industry.

Fifth, improved and liberalized provisions for hospitalization, for rehabilitation, for medical care of disabled members of the armed forces and the merchant marine.

And finally, sufficient pensions for disabled members of the armed forces.

Your government is drawing up other serious, constructive plans for certain immediate forward moves. They concern food, manpower, and other domestic problems that tie in with our armed forces.

Within a few weeks I shall speak with you again in regard to definite actions to be taken by the executive branch of the government, and specific recommendations for new legislation by the Congress.

All our calculations for the future, however, must be based on clear understanding of the problems involved. And that can be gained only by straight thinking—not guesswork, not political manipulation.

I confess that I myself am sometimes bewildered by conflicting statements that I see in the press. One day I read an "authoritative" statement that we shall win the war this year, 1943—and the next day comes another statement equally "authoritative," that the war will still be going on in 1949.

Of course, both extremes—of optimism and pessimism—are wrong.

The length of the war will depend upon the uninterrupted continuance of all-out effort on the fighting fronts and here at home, and that effort is all one.

The American soldier does not like the necessity of waging war. And yet—if he lays off for one single instant he may lose his own life and sacrifice the lives of his comrades.

By the same token—a worker here at home may not like the driving, wartime conditions under which he has to work and live. And yet—if he gets complacent or indifferent and slacks on his job, he too may sacrifice the lives of American soldiers and contribute to the loss of an important battle.

The next time anyone says to you that this war is "in the bag," or says "it's all over but the shouting," you should ask him these questions:

"Are you working full time on your job?"

"Are you growing all the food you can?"

"Are you buying your limit of war bonds?"

"Are you loyally and cheerfully cooperating with your government in preventing inflation and profiteering, and in making rationing work with fairness to all?"

"Because—if your answer is 'No'—then the war is going to last a lot longer than you think.[2]

The plans we made for the knocking out of Mussolini and his gang have largely succeeded. But we still have to knock out Hitler and his gang, and Tojo and his gang. No one of us pretends that this will be an easy matter.

We still have to defeat Hitler and Tojo on their own home grounds. But this will require a far greater concentration of our national energy and our ingenuity and our skill.

It is not too much to say that we must pour into this war the entire strength and intelligence and will power of the United States. We are a great nation—a rich nation—but we are not so great or so rich that we can afford to waste our substance or the lives or our men by relaxing along the way.

We shall not settle for less than total victory. That is the determination of every American on the fighting fronts. That must be, and will be, the determination of every American here at home.

September 8, 1943.

My Fellow Americans:

Once upon a time, a few years ago, there was a city in our Middle West which was threatened by a destructive flood in the great river. The waters had risen to the top of the banks. Every man, woman and child in that city was called upon to fill sand bags in order to defend their homes against the rising waters. For many days and nights, destruction and death stared them in the face.

As a result of the grim, determined community effort, that city still stands. Those people kept the levees above the peak of the flood. All of them joined together in the desperate job that had to be done—business men, workers, farmers, and doctors, and preachers—people of all races.

To me, that town is a living symbol of what community cooperation can accomplish.

Today, in the same kind of community effort, only very much larger, the United Nations and their peoples have kept the levees of civilization high enough to prevent the floods of aggression and barbarism and wholesale murder from engulfing us all. The flood has been raging for four years. At last we are beginning to gain on it; but the waters have not yet receded enough for us to relax our sweating work with the sand bags. In this war bond campaign we are filling bags and placing them against the flood—bags which are essential if we are to stand off the ugly torrent which is trying to sweep us all away.

Today, it is announced that an armistice with Italy has been concluded.

This was a great victory for the United Nations—but it was also a great victory for the Italian people. After years of war and suffering and degradation, the Italian people are at last coming to the day of liberation from their real enemies, the Nazis.

But let us not delude ourselves that this armistice means the end of the war in the Mediterranean. We still have to drive the Germans out of Italy as we have driven them out of Tunisia and Sicily; we must drive them out of France and all other captive countries; and we must strike them on their own soil from all directions.

Our ultimate objectives in this war continue to be Berlin and Tokyo.

I ask you to bear these objectives constantly in mind—and do not forget that we still have a long way to go before we attain them.

The great news that you have heard today from General Eisenhower does not give you license to settle back in your rocking chairs and say, "Well, that does it. We've got 'em on the run. Now we can start the celebration."

The time for celebration is not yet. And I have a suspicion that when this war does end, we shall not be in a very celebrating mood, a very celebrating frame of mind. I think that our main emotion will be one of grim determination that this shall not happen again.

During the past weeks, Mr. Churchill and I have been in constant conference with the leaders of our combined fighting forces. We have been in constant communication with our fighting Allies, Russian and Chinese, who are prosecuting the war with relentless determination and with conspicuous success on far distant fronts. And Mr. Churchill and I are here together in Washington at this crucial moment.

We have seen the satisfactory fulfillment of plans that were made in Casablanca last January and here in Washington last May. And lately we have made new, extensive plans for the future. But throughout these conferences we have never lost sight of the fact that this war will become bigger and tougher, rather than easier, during the long months that are to come.

This war does not and must not stop for one single instant. Your fighting men know that. Those of them who are moving forward through jungles against lurking Japs—those who are landing at this moment, in barges moving through the dawn up to strange enemy coasts—those who are diving their bombers down on the targets at roof-top level at this moment—every one of these men knows that this war is a full-time job and that it will continue to be that until total victory is won.

And, by the same token, every responsible leader in all the United Nations knows that the fighting goes on twenty-four hours a day, seven days a week, and that any day lost may have to be paid for in terms of months added to the duration of the war.

Every campaign, every single operation in all the campaigns that we plan and carry through must be figured in terms of staggering material costs. We cannot afford to be niggardly with any of our resources, for we shall need all of them to do the job that we have put our shoulder to.

Your fellow Americans have given a magnificent account of themselves—on the battlefields and on the oceans and in the skies all over the world.

Now it is up to you to prove to them that you are contributing your share and more than your share. It is not sufficient to simply to put into War Bonds money which we would normally save. We must put into War Bonds money which we would not normally save. Only then have we done everything that good conscience demands. So it is up to you—up to you, the Americans in the American homes—the very homes which our sons and daughters are working and fighting and dying to preserve.

I know I speak for every man and woman throughout the Americas when I say that we Americans will not be satisfied to send our troops into the fire of the enemy with equipment inferior in any way. Nor will we be satisfied to send our troops with equipment only equal to that of the enemy. We are determined to provide our troops with overpowering superiority—superiority of quantity and quality in any and every category of arms and armaments that they may conceivably need.

And where does this our dominating power come from? Why, it can come only from you. The money you lend and the money you give in taxes buys that death-dealing, and at the same time life-saving power that we need for victory. This is an expensive war—expensive in money; you can help it—you can help to keep it at a minimum cost in lives.

The American people will never stop to reckon the cost of redeeming civilization. They know there can never be any economic justification for failing to save freedom.

We can be sure that our enemies will watch this drive with the keenest interest. They know that success in this undertaking will shorten the war. They know that the more money the American people lend to their government, the more powerful and relentless will be the American forces in the field. They know that only a united and determined America could possibly produce on a voluntary basis so huge a sum of money as fifteen billion dollars.

The overwhelming success of the Second War Loan Drive last April showed that the people of this Democracy stood firm behind their troops.

This Third War Loan, which we are starting tonight, will also succeed—because the American people will not permit it to fail.

I cannot tell you how much to invest in War Bonds during this Third War Loan Drive. No one can tell you. It is for you to decide under the guidance of your own conscience.

I will say this, however. Because the nation's needs are greater than ever before, our sacrifices too must be greater than they have ever been before.

Nobody knows when total victory will come—but we do know that the harder we fight now, the more might and power we direct at the enemy now, the shorter the war will be and the smaller the sum total of sacrifice.

Success of the Third War Loan will be the symbol that America does not propose to rest on its arms—that we know the tough, bitter job ahead and will not stop until we have finished it.

Now it is your turn!

Every dollar that you invest in the Third War Loan is your personal message of defiance to our common enemies—to the ruthless savages of Germany and

Japan—and it is your personal message of faith and good cheer to our Allies and to all the men at the front. God bless them!

December 24, 1943.

My Friends:

I have recently returned from extensive journeying in the region of the Mediterranean and as far as the borders of Russia. I have conferred with the leaders of Britain and Russia and China on military matters of the present—especially on plans for stepping- up our successful attack on our enemies as quickly as possible and from many different points of the compass.

On this Christmas Eve there are over 10,000,000 men in the armed forces of the United States alone. One year ago 1,700,000 were serving overseas. Today, this figure has been more than doubled to 3,800,000 on duty overseas. By next July first that number overseas will rise to over 5,000,000 men and women.

That this is truly a World War was demonstrated to me when arrangements were being made with our overseas broadcasting agencies for the time to speak today to our soldiers, and sailors, and marines and merchant seamen in every part of the world. In fixing the time for this broadcast, we took into consideration that at this moment here in the United States, and in the Caribbean and on the Northeast Coast of South America, it is afternoon. In Alaska and in Hawaii and the mid-Pacific, it is still morning. In Iceland, in Great Britain, in North Africa, in Italy and the Middle East, it is now evening.

In the Southwest Pacific, in Australia, in China and Burma and India, it is already Christmas Day. So we can correctly say that at this moment, in those far eastern parts where Americans are fighting, today is tomorrow.

But everywhere throughout the world—throughout this war that covers the world—there is a special spirit that has warmed our hearts since our earliest childhood—a spirit that brings us close to our homes, our families, our friends and neighbors—the Christmas spirit of "peace on earth, good will toward men." It is an unquenchable spirit.

During the past years of international gangsterism and brutal aggression in Europe and in Asia, our Christmas celebrations have been darkened with apprehension for the future. We have said, "Merry Christmas—a Happy New

Year," but we have known in our hearts that the clouds which have hung over our world have prevented us from saying it with full sincerity and conviction.

And even this year, we still have much to face in the way of further suffering, and sacrifice, and personal tragedy. Our men, who have been through the fierce battles in the Solomons, and the Gilberts, and Tunisia and Italy know, from their own experience and knowledge of modern war, that many bigger and costlier battles are still to be fought.

But—on Christmas Eve this year—I can say to you that at last we may look forward into the future with real, substantial confidence that, however great the cost, "peace on earth, good will toward men" can be and will be realized and ensured. This year I *can* say that. Last year I could *not* do more than express a hope. Today I express a certainty—though the cost may be high and the time may be long.

Within the past year—within the past few weeks—history has been made, and it is far better history for the whole human race than any that we have known, or even dared to hope for, in these tragic times through which we pass.

A great beginning was made in the Moscow conference last October by Mr. Molotov, Mr. Eden and our own Mr. Hull. There and then the way was paved for the later meetings.

At Cairo and Teheran we devoted ourselves not only to military matters; we devoted ourselves also to consideration of the future—to plans for the kind of world which alone can justify all the sacrifices of this war.

Of course, as you all know, Mr. Churchill and I have happily met many times before, and we know and understand each other very well. Indeed, Mr. Churchill has become known and beloved by many millions of Americans, and the heartfelt prayers of all of us have been with this great citizen of the world in his recent serious illness.

The Cairo and Teheran conferences, however, gave me my first opportunity to meet the Generalissimo, Chiang Kai-shek, and Marshal Stalin—and to sit down at the table with these unconquerable men and talk with them face to face. We had planned to talk to each other across the table at Cairo and Teheran; but we soon found that we were all on the same side of the table. We came to the conferences with faith in each other. But we needed the personal contact. And now we have supplemented faith with definite knowledge.

It was well worth traveling thousands of miles over land and sea to bring about this personal meeting, and to gain the heartening assurance that we are absolutely agreed with one another on all the major objectives—and on the military means of obtaining them.

At Cairo, Prime Minister Churchill and I spent four days with the Generalissimo, Chiang Kai-shek. It was the first time that we had an opportunity to go over the complex situation in the Far East with him personally. We were able not only to settle upon definite military strategy, but also to discuss certain long-range principles which we believe can assure peace in the Far East for many generations to come.

Those principles are as simple as they are fundamental. They involve the restoration of stolen property to its rightful owners, and the recognition of the rights of millions of people in the Far East to build up their own forms of self-government without molestation. Essential to all peace and security in the Pacific and in the rest of the world is the permanent elimination of the Empire of Japan as a potential force of aggression. Never again must our soldiers and sailors and marines—and other soldiers, sailors and marines—be compelled to fight from island to island as they are fighting so gallantly and so successfully today.

Increasingly powerful forces are now hammering at the Japanese at many points over an enormous arc which curves down through the Pacific from the Aleutians to the Jungles of Burma. Our own Army and Navy, our Air Forces, the Australians and New Zealanders, the Dutch, and the British land, air and sea forces are all forming a band of steel which is slowly but surely closing in on Japan.

On the mainland of Asia, under the Generalissimo's leadership, the Chinese ground and air forces augmented by American air forces are playing a vital part in starting the drive which will push the invaders into the sea.

Following out the military decisions at Cairo, General Marshall has just flown around the world and has had conferences with General MacArthur and Admiral Nimitz—conferences which will spell plenty of bad news for the Japs in the not too far distant future.

I met in the Generalissimo a man of great vision, great courage, and a remarkably keen understanding of the problems of today and tomorrow. We discussed all the manifold military plans for striking at Japan with decisive force from many directions, and I believe I can say that he returned to Chungking with the positive assurance of total victory over our common enemy. Today we and the Republic of China are closer together than ever before in deep friendship and in unity of purpose.

After the Cairo conference, Mr. Churchill and I went by airplane to Teheran. There we met with Marshal Stalin. We talked with complete frankness on every conceivable subject connected with the winning of the war and the establishment of a durable peace after the war.

Within three days of intense and consistently amicable discussions, we agreed on every point concerned with the launching of a gigantic attack upon Germany.

The Russian army will continue its stern offensives on Germany's Eastern front, the allied armies in Italy and Africa will bring relentless pressure on Germany from the south, and now the encirclement will be complete as great American and British forces attack from other points of the compass.

The Commander selected to lead the combined attack from these other points is General Dwight D. Eisenhower. His performances in Africa, in Sicily and in Italy have been brilliant. He knows by practical and successful experience the way to coordinate air, sea and land power. All of these will be under his control. Lieutenant General Carl D. Spaatz will command the entire American strategic bombing force operating against Germany.

General Eisenhower gives up his command in the Mediterranean to a British officer whose name is being announced by Mr. Churchill. We now pledge that new Commander that our powerful ground, sea and air forces in the vital Mediterranean area will stand by his side until every objective in that bitter theatre is attained.

Both of these new Commanders will have American and British subordinate Commanders whose names will be announced to the world in a few days.

During the last two days at Teheran, Marshal Stalin, Mr. Churchill and I looked ahead—ahead to the days and months and years that will follow Germany's defeat. We were united in determination that Germany must be stripped of her military might and be given no opportunity within the foreseeable future to regain that might.

The United Nations have no intention to enslave the German people. We wish them to have a normal chance to develop, in peace, as useful and respectable members of the European family. But we most certainly emphasize that word "respectable"—for we intend to rid them once and for all of Nazism and Prussian militarism and the fantastic and disastrous notion that they constitute the "Master Race."

We did discuss international relationships from the point of view of big, broad objectives, rather than details. But on the basis of what we did discuss, I can say even today that I do not think any insoluble differences will arise among Russia, Great Britain and the United States.

In these conferences we were concerned with basic principles—principles which involve the security and the welfare and the standard of living or human beings in countries large and small.

To use an American and somewhat ungrammatical colloquialism, I may say that I "got along fine" with Marshal Stalin. He is a man who combines a tremendous, relentless determination with a stalwart good humor. I believe he is truly representative of the heart and soul of Russia; and I believe that we are going to get along very well with him and the Russian people—very well indeed.

Britain, Russia, China and the United States and their Allies represent more than three-quarters of the total population of the earth. As long as these four nations with great military power stick together in determination to keep the peace there will be no possibility of an aggressor nation arising to start another world war.

But those four powers must be united with and cooperate with all the freedom-loving peoples of Europe, and Asia, and Africa and the Americas. The rights of every nation, large or small, must be respected and guarded as jealously as are the rights of every individual within our own republic.

The doctrine that the strong shall dominate the weak is the doctrine of our enemies—and we reject it.

But, at the same time, we are agreed that if force is necessary to keep international peace, international force will be applied—for as long as it may be necessary.

It has been our steady policy—and it is certainly a common sense policy—that the right of each nation to freedom must be measured by the willingness of that nation to fight for freedom. And today we salute our unseen Allies in occupied countries—the underground resistance groups and the armies of liberation. They will provide potent forces against our enemies, when the day of the counter- invasion comes.

Through the development of science the world has become so much smaller that we have had to discard the geographical yardsticks of the past. For instance, through our early history the Atlantic and Pacific Oceans were believed to be walls of safety for the United States. Time and distance made it physically possible, for example, for us and for the other American Republics to obtain and maintain our independence against infinitely stronger powers. Until recently very few people, even military experts, thought that the day would ever come when we might have to defend our Pacific Coast against Japanese threats of invasion.

At the outbreak of the first World War relatively few people thought that our ships and shipping would be menaced by German submarines on the high seas or that the German militarists would ever attempt to dominate any nation outside of central Europe.

After the Armistice in 1918, we thought and hoped that the militaristic philosophy of Germany had been crushed; and being full of the milk of human kindness we spent the next twenty years disarming, while the Germans whined so pathetically that the other nations permitted them—and even helped them—to rearm.

For too many years we lived on pious hopes that aggressor and warlike nations would learn and understand and carry out the doctrine of purely voluntary peace.

The well-intentioned but ill-fated experiments of former years did not work. It is my hope that we will not try them again. No—that is putting it too weakly—it is my intention to do all that I humanly can as President and Commander-in-Chief to see to it that these tragic mistakes shall not be made again.

There have always been cheerful idiots in this country who believed that there would be no more war for us, if everybody in America would only return into their homes and lock their front doors behind them. Assuming that their motives were of the highest, events have shown how unwilling they were to face the facts.

The overwhelming majority of all the people in the world want peace. Most of them are fighting for the attainment of peace—not just a truce, not just an armistice—but peace that is as strongly enforced and as durable as mortal man can make it. If we are willing to fight for peace now, is it not good logic that we should use force if necessary, in the future, to keep the peace?

I believe, and I think I can say, that the other three great nations who are fighting so magnificently to gain peace are in complete agreement that we must be prepared to keep the peace by force. If the people of Germany and Japan are made to realize thoroughly that the world is not going to let them break out again, it is possible, and, I hope, probable, that they will abandon the philosophy of aggression—the belief that they can gain the whole world even at the risk of losing their own souls.

I shall have more to say about the Cairo and Teheran conferences when I make my report to the Congress in about two weeks' time. And, on that occasion, I shall also have a great deal to say about certain conditions here at home.

But today I wish to say that in all my travels, at home and abroad, it is the sight of our soldiers and sailors and their magnificent achievements which have given me the greatest inspiration and the greatest encouragement for the future.

To the members of our armed forces, to their wives, mothers and fathers, I want to affirm the great faith and confidence that we have in General Marshall and in Admiral King who direct all of our armed might throughout the world. Upon them falls the great responsibility of planning the strategy of determining where and when we shall fight. Both of these men have already gained high places in American history, places which will record in that history many evidences of their military genius that cannot be published today.

Some of our men overseas are now spending their third Christmas far from home. To them and to all others overseas or soon to go overseas, I can give assurance that it is the purpose of their government to win this war and to bring them home at the earliest possible time.

We here in the United States had better be sure that when our soldiers and sailors do come home they will find an America in which they are given full opportunities for education, and rehabilitation, social security, and employment and business enterprise under the free American system—and that they will find a government which, by their votes as American citizens, they have had a full share in electing.

The American people have had every reason to know that this is a tough and destructive war. On my trip abroad, I talked with many military men who had faced our enemies in the field. These hard-headed realists testify to the strength and skill and resourcefulness of the enemy generals and men whom we must beat before final victory is won. The war is now reaching the stage where we shall all have to look forward to large casualty lists—dead, wounded and missing.

War entails just that. There is no easy road to victory. And the end is not yet in sight.

I have been back only for a week. It is fair that I should tell you my impression. I think I see a tendency in some of our people here to assume a quick ending of the war—that we have already gained the victory. And, perhaps as a result of this false reasoning, I think I discern an effort to resume or even encourage an outbreak of partisan thinking and talking. I hope I am wrong. For, surely, our first and most foremost tasks are all concerned with winning the war and winning a just peace that will last for generations.

The massive offensives which are in the making both in Europe and the Far East—will require every ounce of energy and fortitude that we and our Allies can summon on the fighting fronts and in all the workshops at home. As I have said before, you cannot order up a great attack on a Monday and demand that it be delivered on Saturday.

Less than a month ago I flew in a big Army transport plane over the little town of Bethlehem, in Palestine.

Tonight, on Christmas Eve, all men and women everywhere who love Christmas are thinking of that ancient town and of the star of faith that shone there more than nineteen centuries ago.

American boys are fighting today in snow-covered mountains, in malarial jungles, on blazing deserts; they are fighting on the far stretches of the sea and above the clouds, and fighting for the thing for which they struggle. I think it is best symbolized by the message that came out of Bethlehem.

On behalf of the American people—your own people—I send this Christmas message to you, to you who are in our armed forces:

In our hearts are prayers for you and for all your comrades in arms who fight to rid the world of evil.

We ask God's blessing upon you—upon your fathers, mothers, wives and children—all your loved ones at home.

We ask that the comfort of God's grace shall be granted to those who are sick and wounded, and to those who are prisoners of war in the hands of the enemy, waiting for the day when they will again be free.

And we ask that God receive and cherish those who have given their lives, and that He keep them in honor and in the grateful memory of their countrymen forever.

God bless all of you who fight our battles on this Christmas Eve.

God bless us all. Keep us strong in our faith that we fight for a better day for humankind—here and everywhere.

June 5, 1944.

My Friends:

Yesterday, on June fourth, 1944, Rome fell to American and Allied troops. The first of the Axis capitals is now in our hands. One up and two to go!

It is perhaps significant that the first of these capitals to fall should have the longest history of all of them. The story of Rome goes back to the time of the foundations of our civilization. We can still see there monuments of the time when Rome and the Romans controlled the whole of the then known world. That, too, is significant, for the United Nations are determined that in the future no one city and no one race will be able to control the whole of the world.

In addition to the monuments of the older times, we also see in Rome the great symbol of Christianity, which has reached into almost every part of the world. There are other shrines and other churches in many places, but the churches and shrines of Rome are visible symbols of the faith and determination of the early saints and martyrs that Christianity should live and become universal. And tonight it will be a source of deep satisfaction that the freedom of the Pope and the Vatican City is assured by the armies of the United Nations.

It is also significant that Rome has been liberated by the armed forces of many nations. The American and British armies—who bore the chief burdens of battle—found at their sides our own North American neighbors, the gallant Canadians. The fighting New Zealanders from the far South Pacific, the courageous French and the French Moroccans, the South Africans, the Poles and the East Indians—all of them fought with us on the bloody approaches to the city of Rome.

The Italians, too, forswearing a partnership in the Axis which they never desired, have sent their troops to join us in our battles against the German trespassers on their soil.

The prospect of the liberation of Rome meant enough to Hitler and his generals to induce them to fight desperately at great cost of men and materials and with great sacrifice to their crumbling Eastern line and to their Western front. No thanks are due to them if Rome was spared the devastation which the Germans wreaked on Naples and other Italian cities. The Allied general maneuvered so skillfully that the Nazis could only have stayed long enough to damage Rome at the risk of losing their armies.

But Rome is of course more than a military objective.

Ever since before the days of the Caesars, Rome has stood as a symbol of authority. Rome was the Republic. Rome was the Empire. Rome was and is in a sense the Catholic Church, and Rome was the capital of a United Italy. Later, unfortunately, a quarter of a century ago, Rome became the seat of Fascism—one of the three capitals of the Axis.

For this quarter century the Italian people were enslaved. They were degraded by the rule of Mussolini from Rome. They will mark its liberation with deep emotion. In the north of Italy, the people are still dominated and threatened by the Nazi overlords and their Fascist puppets.

Our victory comes at an excellent time, while our Allied forces are poised for another strike at western Europe—and while the armies of other Nazi soldiers nervously await our assault. And in the meantime our gallant Russian Allies continue to make their power felt more and more.

From a strictly military standpoint, we had long ago accomplished certain of the main objectives of our Italian campaign—the control of the islands—the major islands—the control of the sea lanes of the Mediterranean to shorten our combat and supply lines, and the capture of the airports, such as the great airports of Foggia, south of Rome, from which we have struck telling blows on the continent—the whole of the continent all the way up to the Russian front.

It would be unwise to inflate in our own minds the military importance of the capture of Rome. We shall have to push through a long period of greater effort and fiercer fighting before we get into Germany itself. The Germans have retreated thousands of miles, all the way from the gates of Cairo, through Libya and Tunisia and Sicily and Southern Italy. They have suffered heavy losses, but not great enough yet to cause collapse.

Germany has not yet been driven to surrender. Germany has not yet been driven to the point where she will be unable to recommence world conquest a generation hence.

Therefore, the victory still lies some distance ahead. That distance will be covered in due time—have no fear of that. But it will be tough and it will be costly, as I have told you many, many times.

In Italy the people had lived so long under the corrupt rule of Mussolini that, in spite of the tinsel at the top—you have seen the pictures of him— their economic condition had grown steadily worse. Our troops have found starvation, malnutrition, disease, a deteriorating education and lowered public health—all by-products of the Fascist misrule.

The task of the Allies in occupation has been stupendous. We have had to start at the very bottom, assisting local governments to reform on democratic lines. We have had to give them bread to replace that which was stolen out of their mouths by the Germans. We have had to make it possible for the Italians to raise and use their own local crops. We have to help them cleanse their schools of Fascist trappings.

I think the American people as a whole approve the salvage of these human beings, who are only now learning to walk in a new atmosphere of freedom.

Some of us may let our thoughts run to the financial cost of it. Essentially it is what we can call a form of relief. And at the same time, we hope that this relief will be an investment for the future—an investment that will pay dividends by eliminating Fascism, by ending any Italian desires to start another war of aggression in the future. And that means that they are dividends which justify such an investment, because they are additional supports for world peace.

The Italian people are capable of self-government. We do not lose sight of their virtues as a peace-loving nation.

We remember the many centuries in which the Italians were leaders in the arts and sciences, enriching the lives of all mankind.

We remember the great sons of the Italian people—Galileo and Marconi, Michelangelo and Dante—and incidentally that fearless discoverer who typifies the courage of Italy—Christopher Columbus.

Italy cannot grow in stature by seeking to build up a great militaristic empire. Italians have been overcrowded within their own territories, but they do not need to try to conquer the lands of other peoples in order to find the breath of life. Other peoples may not want to be conquered.

In the past, Italians have come by the millions into the United States. They have been welcomed, they have prospered, they have become good citizens, community and governmental leaders. They are not Italian-Americans. They are Americans—Americans of Italian descent.

The Italians have gone in great numbers to the other Americas—Brazil and the Argentine, for example—hundreds and hundreds of thousands of them. They have gone to many other nations in every continent of the world, giving of their industry and their talents, and achieving success and the comfort of good living, and good citizenship.

Italy should go on as a great mother nation, contributing to the culture and the progress and the good will of all mankind—developing her special talents in the arts and crafts and sciences, and preserving her historic and cultural heritage for the benefit of all peoples.

We want and expect the help of the future Italy toward lasting peace. All the other nations opposed to Fascism and Nazism ought to help to give Italy a chance.

The Germans, after years of domination in Rome, left the people in the Eternal City on the verge of starvation. We and the British will do and are doing everything we can to bring them relief. Anticipating the fall of Rome, we made preparations to ship food supplies to the city, but, of course, it should be borne in mind that the needs are so great, the transportation requirements of our armies so heavy, that improvement must be gradual. But we have already begun to save the lives of the men, women and children of Rome.

This, I think, is an example of the efficiency of your machinery of war. The magnificent ability and energy of the American people in growing the crops, building the merchant ships, in making and collecting the cargoes, in getting the supplies over thousands of miles of water, and thinking ahead to meet emergencies—all this spells, I think, an amazing efficiency on the part of our armed forces, all the various agencies working with them, and American industry and labor as a whole.

No great effort like this can be a hundred percent perfect, but the batting average is very, very high.

And so I extend the congratulations and thanks tonight of the American people to General Alexander, who has been in command of the whole Italian operation; to our General Clark and General Leese of the Fifth and the Eighth Armies; to General Wilson, the Supreme Allied commander of the Mediterranean theater, to General Devers, his American Deputy; to General Eaker; to Admirals Cunningham and Hewitt; and to all their brave officers and men.

May God bless them and watch over them and over all of our gallant, fighting men.

June 23, 1944.

All our fighting men overseas today have their appointed stations on the far-flung battlefronts of the world. We at home have ours too. We need, we are proud of, our fighting men—most decidedly. But, during the anxious times ahead, let us not forget that they need us too.

It goes almost without saying that we must continue to forge the weapons of victory—the hundreds of thousands of items, large and small, essential to the waging of war. This has been the major task from the very start, and it is still a major task. This is the very worst time for any war worker to think of leaving his machine or to look for a peacetime job.

And it goes almost without saying, too, that we must continue to provide our government with the funds necessary for waging war not only by the payment of taxes—which, after all, is an obligation of American citizenship—but also by the purchase of war bonds—an act of free choice which every citizen has to make for himself under the guidance of his own conscience.

Whatever else any of us may be doing, the purchase of war bonds and stamps is something all of us can do and should do to help win the war.

I am happy to report tonight that it is something which nearly everyone seems to be doing. Although there are now approximately sixty-seven million persons who have or earn some form of income, eighty-one million persons or their children have already bought war bonds. They have bought more than six hundred million individual bonds. Their purchases have totaled more than thirty-two billion dollars. These are the purchases of individual men, women, and children. Anyone who would have said this was possible a few years ago would have been put down as a starry-eyed visionary. But of such visions is the stuff of America fashioned.

Of course, there are always pessimists with us everywhere, a few here and a few there. I am reminded of the fact that after the fall of France in 1940 I asked the Congress for the money for the production by the United States of fifty thousand airplanes that year. Well, I was called crazy—it was said that the figure was fantastic; that it could not be done. And yet today we are building airplanes at the rate of one hundred thousand a year.

There is a direct connection between the bonds you have bought and the stream of men and equipment now rushing over the English Channel for the liberation of Europe. There is a direct connection between your bonds and every part of this global war today.

Tonight, therefore, on the opening of this Fifth War Loan Drive, it is appropriate for us to take a broad look at this panorama of world war, for the success or the failure of the drive is going to have so much to do with the speed with which we can accomplish victory and the peace.

While I know that the chief interest tonight is centered on the English Channel and on the beaches and farms and the cities of Normandy, we should not lose sight of the fact that our armed forces are engaged on other battlefronts all over the world, and that no one front can be considered alone without its proper relation to all.

It is worth while, therefore, to make over-all comparisons with the past. Let us compare today with just two years ago—June, 1942. At that time Germany was in control of practically all of Europe, and was steadily driving the Russians back toward the Ural Mountains. Germany was practically in control of North Africa and the Mediterranean, and was beating at the gates of the Suez Canal and the route to India. Italy was still an important military and supply factor—as subsequent, long campaigns have proved.

Japan was in control of the western Aleutian Islands; and in the South Pacific was knocking at the gates of Australia and New Zealand—and also was threatening India. Japan had seized control of most of the Central Pacific.

American armed forces on land and sea and in the air were still very definitely on the defensive, and in the building-up stage. Our allies were bearing the heat and the brunt of the attack.

In 1942 Washington heaved a sigh of relief that the first war bond issue had been cheerfully oversubscribed by the American people. Way back in those days, two year ago, America was still hearing from many "amateur strategists" and political critics, some of whom were doing more good for Hitler than for the United States—two years ago.

But today we are on the offensive all over the world—bringing the attack to our enemies.

In the Pacific, by relentless submarine and naval attacks, and amphibious thrusts, and ever-mounting air attack, we have deprived the Japs of the power to check the momentum of our ever-growing and ever-advancing military forces. We have reduced the Japs' shipping by more than three million tons. We have overcome their original advantage in the air. We have cut off from a return to the homeland tens of thousands of beleaguered Japanese troops who now face starvation or ultimate surrender. And we have cut down their naval strength, so that for many months they have avoided all risk of encounter with our naval forces.

True, we still have a long way to go to Tokyo. But, carrying out our original strategy of eliminating our European enemy first and then turning all our strength to the Pacific, we can force the Japanese to unconditional surrender or to national suicide much more rapidly than has been thought possible.

Turning now to our enemy who is first on the list for destruction—Germany has her back against the wall—in fact three walls at once!

In the south—we have broken the German hold on central Italy. On June 4, the city of Rome fell to the Allied armies. And allowing the enemy no respite, the Allies are now pressing hard on the heels of the Germans as they retreat northwards in ever-growing confusion.

On the east—our gallant Soviet allies have driven the enemy back from the lands which were invaded three years ago. The great Soviet armies are now initiating crushing blows.

Overhead—vast Allied air fleets of bombers and fighters have been waging a bitter air war over Germany and Western Europe. They have had two major objectives: to destroy German war industries which maintain the German armies and air forces; and to shoot the German Luftwaffe out of the air. As a result, German production has been whittled down continuously, and the German fighter forces now have only a fraction of their former power.

This great air campaign, strategic and tactical, is going to continue—with increasing power.

And on the west—the hammer blow which struck the coast of France last Tuesday morning, less than a week ago, was the culmination of many months of careful planning and strenuous preparation.

Millions of tons of weapons and supplies, and hundreds of thousands of men assembled in England, are now being poured into the great battle in Europe.

I think that from the standpoint of our enemy we have achieved the impossible. We have broken through their supposedly impregnable wall in northern France. But the assault has been costly in men and costly in materials. Some of our landings were desperate adventures; but from advices received so far, the losses were lower than our commanders had estimated would occur. We have established a firm foothold. We are now prepared to meet the inevitable counterattacks of the Germans—with power and with confidence. And we all pray that we will have far more, soon, than a firm foothold.

Americans have all worked together to make this day possible.

The liberation forces now streaming across the Channel, and up the beaches and through the fields and the forests of France are using thousands and thousands of planes and ships and tanks and heavy guns. They are carrying with them many thousands of items needed for their dangerous, stupendous undertaking. There is a shortage of nothing—nothing! And this must continue.

What has been done in the United States since those days of 1940—when France fell—in raising and equipping and transporting our fighting forces, and in producing weapons and supplies for war, has been nothing short of a miracle. It was largely due to American teamwork—teamwork among capital and labor and agriculture, between the armed forces and the civilian economy—indeed among all of them.

And every one—every man or woman or child—who bought a war bond helped—and helped mightily!

There are still many people in the United States who have not bought war bonds, or who have not bought as many as they can afford. Everyone knows for himself whether he falls into that category or not. In some cases his neighbors know too. To the consciences of those people, this appeal by the President of the United States is very much in order.

For all of the things which we use in this war, everything we send to our fighting allies, costs money—a lot of money. One sure way every man, woman, and child can keep faith with those who have given, and are giving, their lives, is to provide the money which is needed to win the final victory.

I urge all Americans to buy war bonds without stint. Swell the mighty chorus to bring us nearer to victory!

BIBLIOBAZAAR

The essential book market!

Did you know that you can get any of our titles in large print?

Did you know that we have an ever-growing collection of books in many languages?

Order online:
www.bibliobazaar.com

Find all of your favorite classic books!

Stay up to date with the latest government reports!

At BiblioBazaar, we aim to make knowledge more accessible by making thousands of titles available to you- *quickly and affordably.*

Contact us:
BiblioBazaar
PO Box 21206
Charleston, SC 29413

150612